Catholics and Sex

Kate Saunders is a regular contributor to the *Sunday Times*, *Cosmopolitan* and many other newspapers. She is working on her third novel, *Night Shall Overtake Us*, to be published in late 1992. She was one of the Booker Prize judges in 1990.

Peter Stanford was editor of the *Catholic Herald* for four years, is the author of *Believing Bishops* (Faber, 1990), and a regular contributor to the *Guardian* and the *Independent*. He is writing a biography of Lord Longford for Heinemann.

D1393120

Also by Peter Stanford

Believing Bishops
Hidden Hands

Also by Kate Saunders

The Prodigal Father
Storm in the Citadel

Kate Saunders and Peter Stanford

Catholics and Sex

From Purity to Perdition

'O ye hard hearts, ye cruel men of Rome'
Shakespeare *Julius Caesar*

Mandarin

A Mandarin Paperback
CATHOLICS AND SEX

First published in Great Britain 1992
by William Heinemann Limited
This edition published 1992
by Mandarin Paperbacks
Michelin House, 81 Fulham Road, London SW3 6RB

Mandarin is an imprint of the Octopus Publishing Group,
a division of Reed International Books Limited

Copyright © Kate Saunders and Peter Stanford 1992

A CIP catalogue record for this title
is available from the British Library
ISBN 0 7493 1031 6

Printed and bound in Great Britain
by Cox and Wyman Limited, Reading, Berks

Contents

To the people who spoke out to us
but couldn't give their names

Preface

Roman Catholics are always one screw away from perdition. For centuries, Catholic believers have grown up with the idea that any sexual activity outside the limits laid down by their Church will irredeemably blacken their immortal souls. Even a naughty thought can be enough to trap the spirit in its shameful prison of human flesh.

Most Christian denominations share the Catholic mistrust of sexuality. And because western civilisation has been shaped by Christianity, most of our contemporary assumptions about sex can be traced back to the rulings of the medieval Church. However, although society at large has undergone a scientific and social revolution over the past hundred years, the Catholic Church remains firmly rooted in its medieval past.

Up to now, the world's 919 million Catholics have had two options – remain within the fold and observe the strict sexual rules or leave it and risk eternal damnation. That, at least, is still the official version. But a new generation, feeling that the Church is ludicrously at odds with the rest of society, is agitating for a fundamental change of attitude to sexual morality. Unofficially, the deep divisions between liberal and conservative are pushing the Church towards what one former priest describes as 'the gravest crisis since the Reformation'.[1]

'Conservative thinkers,' writes the Oxford Professor Basil Mitchell, 'see the decline of the formal authority and public influences of the churches in western societies as a problem, to be thought of in terms of decay or disintegration; whereas liberals, viewing the same process as a natural and healthy development, find a problem only in the reluctance of the churches to adapt themselves to it.'[2]

This book, offensive as it will be to many people, is only a reflection of the unofficial, liberal view, currently held by countless Catholics. It is neither a scientific survey nor a political manifesto. We have not set out to criticise the basic tenets of the Catholic faith. Both the authors are practising Christians. Peter Stanford is Roman Catholic, and Kate Saunders is one of those strange hybrids known as an Anglo-Catholic. We wrote this book with the footsteps of Francis Thompson's 'The Hound of Heaven' behind us –

> . . . with unhurried chase,
> And unperturbed pace,
> Deliberate speed, majestic instancy,
> They beat – and a Voice beat
> More instant than the Feet –
> 'All things betray thee, who betrayest Me.'[3]

We do not feel, however, that re-examining the Church's sexual morality is a betrayal of heaven. Why is sexual pleasure automatically wrong? Why should believers have to choose between faith in God or a rewarding sex life? How did this state of affairs come about? And – most important – what would happen to the Catholic Church if the concept that sex is wicked were to be abolished? These are the questions we have addressed. We are not proposing moral anarchy, or an end to loving monogamy, but total freedom and fulfilment within relationships.

Of one thing we are absolutely certain: if ever the Pope decided that sex between two consenting adults was not, in itself, a sin, he would declare an amnesty for millions of deeply unhappy 'sinners' and show the world that the true message of Christianity cannot be reduced to what the faithful get up to in their bedrooms.

One:
Catholics and Sex

Adam returned to the kitchen and made the tea. While
waiting for it to draw, he mentally composed a short article:
'Catholicism, Roman' for a Martian encyclopaedia, compiled
after life on earth had been destroyed by atomic warfare.
'Roman Catholicism was, according to archeological evidence,
distributed fairly widely over the planet earth in the twentieth
century. As far as the western hemisphere is concerned, it
appears to have been characterised by a complex system of
sexual taboos and rituals. Other doctrines included a belief in
a divine redeemer and in life after death.'[1]

David Lodge
The British Museum is Falling Down

The sexual act, according to traditional Catholic doctrine, exists
solely for the procreation of children. To indulge in sexual
intercourse purely for pleasure – even if you are married – is a sin
against God. So are contraception, abortion, masturbation and
homosexuality. So is thinking about sex. Even when contemporary Vatican documents speak of the 'sacredness' of married sex
(an attractive concept that rings true in many a Catholic's
experience), that sacredness appears to lie more in its absence
than its presence. Or, to be fair, in the confinement of sex to
certain safe times and approved circumstances.

Once upon a time, these views were taken for granted by the
whole of western society. Times have changed, but the Roman
Catholic Church has not. It clings to the medieval concept of
Natural Law – God made male and female, and invented copulation as the process by which he could create new life in them.

3

To interfere with this process by trying to prevent conception in any way is to break God's law. Animals, with their apparently businesslike, unlustful couplings, hold the clue to what sex was like for Adam and Eve, before they sinned. After all, goes the argument, have you ever seen a mouse practising coitus interruptus or an elephant wanking? No – these sins are confined to fallen humanity. To remain within the law, humans must firstly be married, and secondly see copulation through to its 'natural' conclusion – as Magnus Magnussen would say, a case of 'I've started, so I'll finish.'

This is the basis of Catholic sexual morality, handed down through the generations and overseen to this day by a male, celibate hierarchy. The Church's rules are designed to exercise iron control over the private, personal and emotional area of human existence. And these rules continue to cause untold misery and guilt to those brought up in the Catholic tradition. 'My life has been ruined by them,' says the novelist Wendy Perriam, speaking for countless others. 'Over and above the misery, I feel a terrible anger. The Catholic Church has caused so much anger with its sexual teachings that it ought to declare a special Day of Anger. We would all go into Westminster Cathedral – men who have been beaten up by the Christian Brothers, girls who have been made to feel ashamed of their bodies – and rail against the priests and nuns who did that to us.'

Perriam's proposed *dies irae* may sound a touch drastic, but today's Church needs some way of getting its sexual hang-ups out of its system, to clear the decks for more important issues. The rigor mortis which afflicts the Vatican's sexual morality in this so-called permissive age is beginning to obscure the true power and meaning of Christianity itself. When non-believers increasingly take the statement 'I am a Catholic' as a euphemism for 'I am sexually repressed', it is one more symptom of the Church establishment's failure to place itself in the real world.

This is reality: thousands of people are leaving the Church every year, unable to cope with the ludicrous and unnecessary demands made on their personal lives. Between 1979 and 1989, British RC congregations dropped by 14 per cent. Over the past twenty years, an estimated 100,000 priests have walked away from their vows.[2]

Of course, it would be foolish to claim that sexual morality is the only reason for this mass apostasy. The increasing secularisation of western society puts pressure on many other aspects of religious thinking – for example, the emphasis upon the power of the individual is at odds with the Catholic tradition of submission to authority. The fact that ours is a society that worships science must also be taken into account. When it comes to explaining the laws of the universe, we are far more willing to take the word of a physicist in a white coat than a divine in a Roman collar.

But there is little doubt that many of the faithful are alienated for the most basic, personal reasons. If contraception and abortion are socially acceptable ways of improving the quality of life, the Catholic choice between no sex or fifteen children is only for the super-devout. A priest who processes the laicisations of clergy who have broken their vows tells us that in 99.9 per cent of cases, these priests have deserted their flocks because they fell in love with a woman, and wished to marry her in church. They were not turning their backs on God or the faith – simply the early medieval ruling that priests should be celibate.

The Vatican, the spiritual and legal centre of world Catholicism, is a bureaucracy. Why do cardinals wear red? To match the tape. Down the ages, whenever sexual prejudice has collided with political expediency, it has duly been enshrined in the laws of the Church. In many cases, the laws relating to sexuality were formulated to deal with a specific set of historical circumstances. The Vatican, as God's business address on earth, has no provision for changing the rules when the original circumstances have become obsolete. Instead, successive popes have allowed them to calcify into dogmas, and held them up as eternal truths. Modern society may be starting to accept homosexuality and feminism, but not the Church. Each time the sexual rules are questioned, the Big Birettas of the Vatican reply with more rules, until every Catholic bed wears a barbed-wire duvet.

The result of this complicated evolution is that there are, in many people's minds, two kinds of morality: a: sexual morality b: everything else. Generations of Catholics have been reared on the idea that if they refrain from extra-marital sex and reject contraception, they are living a perfect life. As the writer Frank Delaney says of his upbringing in rural Ireland: 'The one morality in Ireland in those days did not mean cheating people of money, beating them up or murdering them. It meant sexual morality. The attitude to sex stood for barbarism in familial conduct. The bitterness, the lack of charity, the malice, were quite extraordinary.'

Delaney maintains that the Church of his boyhood used its sexual rules to keep the faithful in a state of total submission. 'Sexuality has been focused on because it is such a vulnerable and powerful emotional area. It cries out for control. Analyse the power they have. What do they say to a young couple walking out? You may not touch her breasts. You may not touch his genitals. Why? Because it's a sin. What will happen? You'll fall out of favour with God. If you suddenly die, you're condemned to hellfire. That's the rationale I was brought up with. When you start to scrutinise the system, you realise you are dealing with profound intellectual and moral corruption. The Catholic Church is a political organisation, with a vested interest in keeping up its numbers. It does not count the cost of the emotional damage it causes with these sweeping, dogmatic statements it makes regarding sexuality.'

It is only fair to add that Delaney is talking about a Church that belongs to the past. The reforming and modernising Second Vatican Council of the mid-1960s 'opened a window on the world' in Pope John XXIII's famous phrase. Since then, the Church has undergone massive liberalisation, throwing far more power into the lap of the individual worshipper. It has tackled many of the traditional bugbears of disaffected Catholics, such as the complete lack of sex education in Church schools, and relaxed its rules regarding sex within marriage.

We should also remember that as an Irishman, Delaney grew up with a Church that had (and still has) such a strong grip upon the national culture that many of its rules are enshrined in the constitution. Until a few years ago, it was possible to see Irish priests whacking the bushes outside rural dancehalls, to break up any courting couples. Similarly, in Franco's Spain, in the 1970s, the local priest would sit beside the projector in the cinema, blocking out the love-scenes in the film with a piece of card. The Catholic Churches of Britain, America and France have been far more liberal for far longer, presumably taking their cues from the secular societies around them.

However, wherever a Catholic happens to be born, the official line remains essentially the same – sex is a sin. The Vatican's most recent declaration concerning sexual ethics (1975) made no bones about this: 'In the present period, the corruption of morals has increased, and one of the most serious indications of this corruption is the unbridled exaltation of sex.'[3] Up to a point, this is quite right. A hundred years from now, our era's obsession with sex will probably seem as peculiar as the Victorians' obsession with death. We do bang on about it to an extraordinary degree – the authors would like to bet you are not reading this book because of the word 'Catholics' in the title.

But an obsession with sex is only a symptom of a deeper political issue. The process of liberalisation is bound up with the rights of the individual. And the individual's right to regulate his or her own sexual behaviour is held by liberals to be self-evident. Because this area of life is so nearly concerned with personal freedom, any attempts by a so-called higher authority to curtail it are hotly resented.

The whole question of sexuality touches the heart of the conflict between liberalism and conservatism in the Catholic Church. The Church is a hierarchy, which revolves around the authority of the man who sits upon the Throne of St Peter, Christ's representative on earth. The Second Vatican Council was only prepared to go part of the way down the road to modernity. Recognising its sexual rules as the foundation of its power over the individual, it drew the line at change. Right from the start, the Pope let it be known that the celibacy of priests and nuns would not be discussed.

In 1968, at the end of Vatican II, the hopes of many Catholics were dashed with the publication of the papal encyclical entitled

Humanae Vitae. This marked the limit of reform, with an unequi-vocal ban on artificial contraception provoked by the introduc-tion of the contraceptive pill. Many couples reacted by breaking the tradition of generations and simply ignoring the papal edict. Some argue that the ostrich position adopted by the Vatican in *Humanae Vitae* was the beginning of the end of papal authority; the breaching of the dam.

'If a Catholic couple decided, privately and with a conscience, to use contraceptives,' writes David Lodge, 'there was nothing that priest, bishop or Pope could do to stop them . . . Thus contraception was the issue on which many lay Catholics first attained moral autonomy, rid themselves of superstition, and ceased to regard their religion as, in the moral sphere, an encyclopaedic rule-book in which a clear answer was to be found to every possible question of conduct.'[4]

A 1970s' poll in a Catholic parish in Liverpool found 80 per cent opposed to *Humanae Vitae*. In his 1990 survey 'Roman Catholic Attitudes in Britain', the sociologist Michael Hornsby-Smith could not find one voice raised in unqualified approval of the contraceptive ban.[5] But the unpopularity of *Humanae Vitae* only has the ostriches burying their heads deeper. Pope John Paul II is reportedly on the verge of issuing a new encyclical to reinforce the old one.

True, despite John Paul's ultra-conservative attitude to sexual morality, some of the signals coming out of Rome are more encouraging. It has finally been recognised, for example, that it is possible to enjoy sex without ending up on the devil's barbecue. Sometimes (full moon, fingers crossed, written permission in triplicate) you may even do it without an eye to conceiving more Catholics. Yet John Paul is still telling husbands they are commit-ting a sin if they 'lust'[6] after their wives. Cardinal Ratzinger is still describing homosexuals as fundamentally 'disordered'.[7]

The Vatican's stubborn adherence to its ancient sexual rules can sometimes appear to be beyond all reason. John Paul has often expressed his solidarity with the poorest of his faithful, in poverty-racked, debt-ridden Third World countries. Yet almost in the same breath he exhorts them to hold true to *Humanae*

Vitae, and to oppose any attempts by governments or international agencies to control population. No government, he would maintain, has the right to prevent a couple having a child. Well and good. Where he and the liberals part company is over the rights of couples who wish to have a sexual relationship without producing more mouths they cannot feed.

In prosperous, liberated western society, like it or not, John Paul's sexual prejudices are so wildly out of step with the times that they detract from more important aspects of the Church's message. His laudable attempts, in his encyclicals *Sollicitudo Rei Socialis* (1989) and *Centisimus Annus* (1990), to sketch a third way between the excesses of capitalism and communism have been overshadowed, because of the public image of the Church as standing for sexual pessimism and repression.

David Lodge wrote his Martian's definition of Catholicism in the 1960s, when the debate surrounding the contraceptive pill dominated Church life. But he could equally well have directed his satire at any period of the Church's 2000-year history. Except, of course, the beginning.

The Beginning

In the beginning was the Word. The Word was God, and the Word made flesh was Jesus Christ. It is Christ's death and resurrection, as a covenant with God for human redemption, that is the driving force of the Christian religion. In order to die, you must first be born, and in order to be born, you must be mortal. In order to rise physically from the dead, on the other hand, you must be divine and immortal. One without the other is not, for most denominations, true Christianity; and it is most certainly not Catholicism.

It is, however, one of the oddest aspects of Christianity that while unbelievers find it hard to accept the divinity of Christ, believers have always seemed to have difficulty accepting his humanity. Having human flesh means entering the world through a woman's vagina. It means eating, drinking, excreting and experiencing sexual urges. All the things, in fact, which Christian morality has taught us to regard as degrading or sinful. Only the boldest have dared to wonder whether the Son of God ever had an erection, or – perish the thought – a sexual relationship. Many Christians cannot even bear to think that Christ might have farted during his life on earth.

Yet the whole point of Christianity is that although Christ was God, he was also a man, who shared and understood the demands of the human body. The Son of Man, in his own words, came eating and drinking. He could be hungry, short-tempered and tired. The four Gospels of the New Testament show a vigorous, problematical man, human and superhuman rather than divine and ethereal. Christ's ministry was confined to his last three years on earth. His previous career as a professional carpenter must have required a convincing performance as a human being.

The Gospels of Matthew, Mark, Luke and John never miss an opportunity to portray Christ as a fulfilment of Jewish prophecy. Christ was not only born into the Jewish faith, but was a most learned and devout Jew. And, as such, he drew his morality from Jewish law. The Old Testament is full of complicated sexual rules, mostly relating to hygiene. There is, however, not a trace of the Christian hostility to the sexual act itself. The self-protective tribes of Israel valued the begetting of children too much to advocate chastity. The Roman Tacitus (d. AD 120)[8] commented disapprovingly on the supposed sexual licentiousness of the Jews, and their eagerness to increase their numbers. Christ, as we shall see, wholeheartedly approved of the married state, and seems to have been relaxed and happy among women and small children.

It is always worth remembering that Christ's critical attitude to the Jewish law was based upon a fundamental respect – why bother to change something you believe to be worthless? Critical he was, however, especially when he felt that the law was being observed at the expense of common sense and compassion.

There is a beautiful example of this in the Gospel of St John. A woman has been caught in the act of committing adultery. According to Jewish law, she must be stoned to death. Before stoning her, the Pharisees have brought the woman to Jesus.

> Making her stand there in full view of everybody, they said to Jesus, 'Master, this woman was caught in the very act of committing adultery, and Moses has ordered us in the law to condemn women like this to death by stoning. What have you to say?' They asked him this as a test, looking for something to use against him. But Jesus bent down and started writing on the ground with his finger. As they persisted with their question, he looked up, and said, 'If there is one of you who has not sinned, let him be the first to throw a stone at her.' Then he bent down and wrote on the ground again. When they heard this, they went away one by one, beginning with the eldest, until Jesus was left alone with the woman, who remained standing there. He looked up and said, 'Woman, where are they? Has no one condemned you?'
> 'No one, sir,' she replied.
> 'Neither do I condemn you,' said Jesus. 'Go away, and don't sin any more.'
>
> John 8:3–11

If sexual irregularity is a sin, Jesus shows here that it is ONLY a sin, on a level with every other kind of sin. Throughout the Gospels, moreover, he makes it clear that the business of condemning sins belongs to God, not to humans. (See Luke 6.) Through him, he says, sins may be forgiven, not once but into infinity. Nowhere in the Gospels does he imply that there is any such thing as a person who is irredeemably damaged because of a sin of the flesh.

In fact, there are very few Gospel passages where Christ mentions sins of the flesh at all. David Lodge's Martian would be amazed to discover just how little Christ said about sex, and so would many Catholics. Traditionally, Catholics have been discouraged from reading the Bible themselves. Their knowledge of the Gospels has been drip-fed to them through layers of theologians and priests, because the Church has always been aware of the dangers of individual interpretation. This, like so much else, is now changing, but there are still Catholic adults who would be surprised if they read the New Testament straight through.

They would be brought up sharply against one of the most controversial and disputed passages, in Chapter 19 of the Gospel of St Matthew, which has traditionally been interpreted by theologians as Christ's seal of approval for celibacy. We will be discussing this in detail in a later chapter. For now, it is enough to stress that Christ ended his discourse with the mild observation that 'it is not everyone who can accept what I have said'. For his era, his rare pronouncements on sexual morality are extremely compassionate and liberal. But sex is much further from the core of his teaching than the Church has led us to believe. His true priorities appear to be somewhat different.

> One of the scribes [. . .] put a further question to him, 'Which is the first of all the commandments?' Jesus replied, 'This is the first: Listen, Israel, the Lord our God is the one, only Lord, and you must love the Lord your God with all your heart, with all your soul, with all your mind and with all your strength. The second is this: You must love your neighbour as yourself. There is no commandment greater than these.'[9]

> Mark 12:28–31

These two rules seem to us not merely to permit a liberal interpretation, but to demand it. Are the Catholic priests who scream at young women outside abortion clinics loving their neighbours as themselves?

They might argue that their neighbours, in this case, were the clusters of cells inside the young women's bodies. Or they might justify themselves with the maxim of St Thomas Aquinas: 'We must show our neighbours a holy hatred by loving them for what they are, and hating whatever there is in them that blocks our way to God.'[10]

We venture to suggest that Jesus Christ, as we understand him, would not have considered any kind of hatred holy. The twin themes of compassion and forgiveness chime through the

Gospels as regularly as the Angelus bell. Anyone wishing to prove that sex is a sin would have a hard time finding justification in the recorded sayings of Christ.

The Early Church

So how, exactly, did the Catholic Church get its collective underwear into such a twist about sex? If today's pessimism and hostility can be blamed neither on Christ nor the Judaic tradition, where do we get it from?

Naming the guilty men means unravelling a tangled skein of ancient philosophies and ideologies. To put it in the simplest possible way, Christianity is the point at which the paths of Judaism and the cultures of ancient Greece and Rome meet.

By the first century AD, the notion that sexual pleasure was inherently wicked was already hundreds of years old. Pythagoras (sixth century BC) considered the sexual act unhealthy for men, because it sapped their strength. Women, because they did not ejaculate, suffered no ill-effects. This was a view shared and developed by Plato (d. 348 BC) and his even more influential pupil, Aristotle.

Plato held that the human body was evil, because physical demands distracted the mind from the pursuit of truth. 'The body is the source of endless trouble to us,' he wrote. 'It fills us full of loves, and lusts, and fears, and fancies of all kinds, and endless foolery, and in fact, as men say, takes away from us all powers of thinking at all [. . .] having got rid of the foolishness of the body we shall be pure.'[11]

Aristotle agreed that the sexual functions of the body were degrading and dangerous, and stressed the inferiority of women, as mere vessels for carrying a man's seed. The effects of this ancient Greek's scorn for sexual pleasure can still be felt by the Catholic Church of today, for Aristotle's ideas were Christianised in the thirteenth century by the greatest of all Catholic theologians, St Thomas Aquinas.

Another ancient influence was the philosophical school known as the Stoa, active from 300 BC to AD 250. The Stoics believed that all bodily and earthly pleasures were detrimental to virtue. Seneca, the Stoic appointed tutor to the Emperor Nero in the middle of the first century, set the tone for a thousand papal encyclicals, when he wrote that it was 'shameful to love one's own wife to excess [. . .] nothing can be more depraved than to make love to one's own wife as if she were an adulteress [. . .] provided you remain untouched by the noxious breath of sexual pleasure, every other form of craving, too, will pass you by.'[12] Seneca may have failed to impress his ideas on his notoriously dissolute royal pupil, but his motto 'Nothing for pleasure's sake' has been enthusiastically taken up by generations of Catholics.

Did Jesus Christ hate pleasure? Down the ages, Catholic theologians have been through the Bible with tweezers and magnifying-glasses, in search of proof that he did. The anti-sexuality of the ancients was, by the third century, so deeply etched on the Christian mind that reinventing the character of Christ became an urgent necessity.

One other major strand of thought completes the picture. This is the heresy known as Gnosticism. This movement, called Gnosis (knowledge), is thought to have come from Persia, and many modern liberal theologians (notably the radical German, Uta Ranke Heinemann) maintain that it is, even today, an enduring boil on the Catholic behind.

The Gnostics believed that all matter – the visible world of flesh – was evil, in the grip of an evil creator. Only the spirit, coming from the invisible world of light, was good. Procreation was therefore bad, because it imprisoned one more divine spark in a vile body. Any kind of physical pleasure was bad, because it distracted the soul from its journey back to the light. The fact of existence, far from being a gift of God, meant being a slave to the forces of darkness. Inevitably, the Gnostic interpretation of Christianity emphasised a Christ more divine than human. As Bertrand Russell explains: 'The Gnostics considered it unworthy of the Son of God to be born, to be an infant, and, above all, to die upon the cross; they said that these things had befallen the man

14

Jesus, but not the divine Son of God.'[13] One Gnostic sect, the Docetics, believed that the crucified Christ was a mere ghost, purely spirit.

The early Christian Church fought vigorously against this heresy, but the Gnostics' distaste for sex remains in the Catholic bloodstream like a virus. Every time the Church appears to suggest that Christ's body did not function in a normal, human manner, it can be interpreted as a Gnostic blast from the past. It is no coincidence that St Augustine, arguably the single most influential Catholic writer, came to Christianity via Manichae-ism, a Gnostic sect which rejected marriage, sex and procreation and elevated the state of virginity. Sounds familiar? Yes, we are getting nearer home.

Augustine was born in North Africa in AD 354, the son of a pagan father and a Christian mother, St Monica. He became a Manichaeist in his late teens, and as he tells in his famous *Confessions* lived with a mistress for sixteen years. Under pressure from his saintly mother, he sent this woman away, to prepare for marriage with a 'suitable' young lady. Unable to contain his lust, he took another mistress while he was waiting. His conversion to Christianity in AD 386 filled him with disgust for his wicked ways – which he blamed entirely upon women. It was women who were responsible for inflaming his lust. Sex was fundamentally evil, he declared, and a perfect life could only be lived far away from female influence. In his huge book *City of God*, he laid the foundations of the Catholic misogyny which places the burden of sex on female shoulders. Women are earth, men are spirit. Even within marriage, the sexual act was sinful, and only remotely justifiable when there was an intention to produce children. Virginity was morally streets ahead of marriage.

With Aristotle, Augustine provided St Thomas Aquinas (d. 1274) with the inspiration for his *Summa Theologiae*, which remains the cornerstone of modern Catholic theology. In this massive work, the sexual ethics of the ancient philosophers and the first Christians, with just a dash of Gnosticism thrown in, were finally moulded into one definitive whole. 'Thomas felt assured of Aristotle's posthumous support,' writes Uta Ranke

Heinemann, 'not only for his belittlement of women, but for his hostility to sexual pleasure. Aristotle's assertion that sexual desire hampers thought was grist to his mill and reinforced his Augustinian sexual pessimism.'[14]

Sugar and Spice and all Things Nasty

It is impossible to discuss Catholic sexual pessimism without discussing the Church's hostility to women. Far from being separate issues, they are two sides of the same coin. The Church hates and fears women because women – according to traditional patristic and scholastic theology – are sex.

Alongside the history of the Church runs a parallel history of virulent misogyny and repression of women. Once again, this is not something that can be blamed on Christ. The Gospels are full of examples of his respect for women, and he had many female friends and followers. St Paul's Epistles show that women were active in the early Church.

In Christ's day, Jewish women were chattels, who could be divorced by their husbands for spoiling a dinner or talking to a man in the street. A man could cast off one wife and take another, more or less as the fancy took him. Women did not have the same licence. When Jesus spoke against divorce (Matthew 5 & 19, Luke 16), saying that a married couple were one flesh, joined forever by God, he was therefore advocating a dramatic improvement in women's status.

Even more significantly, Jesus showed that he thought a woman's spiritual development as important as a man's. When he visited his friends, the sisters Martha and Mary of Bethany, Martha complained that she was doing all the work of serving, while Mary sat spellbound at the Master's feet.

> But the Lord answered, 'Martha, Martha,' he said, 'you worry and fret about so many things, and yet few are needed,

indeed only one. It is Mary who has chosen the better part, and it is not to be taken from her.'

Luke 10: 38–42

In other words, he refused to banish Mary to the kitchen, to get on with 'women's work'. (The editors of the New Jerome Biblical Commentary add a cautionary note: 'The lesson is not that one should prepare a casserole rather than a seven-course meal'[15] – presumably in case some housekeeper skimps on Father's Sunday lunch with the excuse that she was busy listening to his sermon.)

Many women were attracted to Christ's ministry, and they were not discouraged from taking an active role. The accepted picture of the twelve male disciples, neatly arranged around the Lord like a set of apostle teaspoons, is far from complete.

> Now it happened that after this he made his way through towns and villages preaching and proclaiming the good news of the Kingdom of God. With him went the Twelve, as well as certain women who had been cured of evil spirits and ailments: Mary, surnamed the Magdalene, from whom seven demons had gone out, Joanna the wife of Herod's steward Chuza, Susanna, and many others who provided for them out of their own resources.

Luke 8: 1–3

Some people would be surprised to learn here that Christ's ministry was effectively bankrolled by female disciples. There are many examples of his friendships with women. It was the women who kept faith with Jesus at the foot of the Cross, when many of the male disciples fled in fear. It was to a woman, Mary Magdalene, that the Son of God first revealed himself after the Resurrection.

St Paul, in his First Epistle to the Corinthians, famously stated that women should 'keep silence' in church.[16] In the same letter, however, he describes women preaching as a commonplace event. He mentions notable Christian women – Phebe, Priscilla and Junia. The earliest Christian Church, it seems, was an exciting and fulfilling place for women.

What went wrong? Only a few centuries later, Christianity was thoroughly infected by the anti-femininity of the ancients. Womanhood was bound up with the 'natural' and disgusting processes of menstruation and childbirth. Spiritually, morally and legally, women were second-class citizens.

And worse. Women were dangerously close to everything vile, corrupt and of the tomb. They represented, in their lust-provoking bodies, the gateway to death and damnation – let innocent men beware. 'The whole of her bodily beauty is nothing less than phlegm, blood, bile, rheum, and the fluid of digested food,' wrote St John Crystostom (AD 347–407). 'If you consider what is stored up behind those lovely eyes, the angle of the nose, the mouth and cheeks you will agree that the well-proportioned body is merely a whitened sepulchre.'[17]

The Catholic Church's obsession with virginity, closely coupled with the unholiness of the normal, mature woman, was well under way. Having sex with one of these pieces of Adam's rib, said theologians, was the equivalent of embracing a bag of shit.

After all, the argument went, let us not forget that the fall of mankind is all Eve's fault. 'I am Eve,' says an old Irish poem, 'the wife of noble Adam; it was I who violated Jesus in the past; it was I who robbed my children of heaven; it is I by right who should have been crucified [. . .] there would be no hell [. . .] but for me.'[18] The lot of women was thought to be deservedly dreadful, as punishment for the crime of the mother of us all.

As ordinary women went down in estimation, however, the cult of one extraordinary woman grew. The Virgin Mary, Mother of God, was increasingly held up as the one perfect created being. Though mentions of Mary in the Gospels are scanty, the Church has erected around her meek, pure and compliant figure a vast scaffolding of legend.

The Church, when accused of misogyny, will often point to the adored figure of the Virgin Mother, whose statue can be found in most churches. At the moment you are reading this, millions of Catholics are murmuring prayers to Mary, begging her to use her influence with her son. She is our Mother, our Star, our Lady of Perpetual Succour, Help of Christians. She is the Queen of Heaven, enthroned in splendour.

As a role model for women, however, she is not only impossible, but a perpetual reproach to the very state of womanhood itself. The Fathers of the Church could not bear the thought of Christ residing in the womb of a woman who had sexual intercourse at any time of her life. Mary had to be different – a Virgin before and after becoming a Mother, herself conceived without sin. The clear implication is that, although Christ was human, ordinary human gestation, inside the body of an ordinary, 'dirty' human woman, was not nearly good enough for him. Never mind the shaky Biblical justification for this miracle – it must have been what God intended! 'In the very celebration of the perfect human woman,' writes Marina Warner, 'both humanity and women were subtly denigrated.'

The Church's attitude to women has modified somewhat, since St John Crysostom set down his barmy utterances. But the modern Church still categorises women as either nuns or whores, with married mothers in the middle, a blend of both. It is still far, far easier for a woman to commit a sexual sin than a man. Her very flesh is wicked, because it can kindle the fires of male lust. Catholic misogyny is intimately bound up with Catholic fear and loathing of sex.

One female theologian goes as far as declaring that the true, subconscious reasoning behind all Catholic sexual rules is a fear of women priests – once you allow contraception, you free women from the restrictions of their biology, and find them demanding powers usually reserved for men. 'The demon of the pagans still haunts the question,' says Marina Warner. 'I think they really are frightened of a return to priestesses – the ancient spectre of the cult of Cybele; mad maenads rushing through the streets, menstruating and tearing their hair.'

These primitive fears have already surfaced in the Church of England, in the debate surrounding women priests. The Anglican experience should give Catholic feminists a fair idea of what they may expect on the far-off day when the question is raised officially in their own Church. Anglican women have heard some amazing nonsense about women's spiritual inferiority and physical uncleanness – the old prejudices die hard.

In both Churches, feminists are claiming that the hostility to women is compounded by homosexual cliques – any organisation that excludes women is bound to attract the type of homosexual who wishes to get away from them. 'Gay priests add a more profound focus to the misogyny of the male club,' says Frances Kissling, head of American Catholics for a Free Choice. Feminists vs. Gays is not a pretty battle to watch. We will be looking at it in more detail later. It is yet another symptom of the Church's disastrous sexual wrongheadedness and confusion.

The most pressing feminist issue, however, remains the ban on artificial contraception. 'The historical reality,' Kissling says, 'is that Church objections in this area are not based on respect for life, but on misogyny, an antipathy to sexuality. Underpinning it is the failure of the Church to see women as moral agents and their sexuality as positive.'

A Catholic journalist told us she left the Church at the age of nineteen, because 'I could only see that it hated me as a woman.' Women have been the backbone of the Church since the Papacy of St Peter. If the Church wishes to keep its female faithful into the next century, however, it would be wise to give them more to do besides having babies, filling convents and making the sandwiches. Feminism has arrived in the outside world. It is high time it penetrated the musty recesses of the Church that Time Forgot.

An Unhealthy Obsession

Drawing up sexual rules is one issue. Enforcing them is another. Many (most) branches of Christianity are equally strict. The Catholic Church, however, has a tradition of priestly intervention between the individual soul and God. For hundreds of years, the Catholic priest has acted as a kind of moral filter-system, scraping off people's worst sins before presenting them to the Almighty. So one should not be surprised to see certain sections of the Church reacting with hysteria, when so many of the faithful are deciding to take responsibility for their own sex lives. Younger, liberal priests are only too glad to be turfed out of the bedroom, but an older generation is still hammering on the door.

Those who defend the Church's right to take such a keen interest in sexual morality would argue that it springs from a vision of the Christian role as standing apart from the world, offering dispassionate guidance from the sidelines. This is one of the traditional reasons for the mandatory celibacy of Catholic clergy – that players can't be referees.

Where sex is concerned, there is a danger that in seeing the world apparently swept away in an orgy of sexual gratification, and in wishing to warn of the perils of this situation, the Church itself has fallen into the trap of making sex far too important.

Bishop Cormac Murphy-O'Connor, head of the Catholic diocese of Arundel and Brighton, feels that Christ's interest in human freedom should be explored in regard to sex. He sees *Humanae Vitae* not only as questioning the morality of artificial contraception, but also as an exploration of the balance between the individual needs of couples to limit their families, and what the so-called 'contraceptive mentality' means to the world at large. 'The Church has to ask,' he says, 'is sex without the pill more in accordance with building a society more imbued with the spirit of the Gospel? The processes of life are very precious. If you start interfering with them, particularly in terms of how they begin in sexual intercourse, then the Church is saying something very important. *Humanae Vitae* wasn't meant to be a question of "if you don't do this, you're damned". Pope Paul VI was asking if Gospel living is bound up with sexuality.'

This is the trillion-dollar question that has replaced 'how many angels can dance on the head of a pin?' in theological circles. Of course, the Church has a duty to defend human life. But how far does this give it a licence to meddle in the natural processes of that life?

'You may repress some individuals,' says the writer Mary Kenny, 'but you save others. In divorce, for example, you may repress some people by your laws, but what about the other side of the question, the children of a marriage in trouble? How do you set their needs against the individual partners' happiness?' Kenny and other traditionalist Catholics maintain that the Church cannot duck out of such issues, or weaken its moral standpoint, without damaging its credibility. One person's repressive rule is another's shining ideal.

Enforcing rules for something as chaotic as sex, however, is fraught with difficulties. Firstly, the rules are drawn up by celibate clerics who are seldom in the position of having to live by them. In the old days, a man gained respect if he never had sex. These days, anyone not getting it tends – rightly or wrongly – to be regarded as pitiful and faintly absurd. Problem number one is a lack of credibility.

Secondly, teenage girls will continue to get pregnant and marriages will continue to bite the dust, whether the Church forbids it or not. The whole dogfight over the rules is an outward and visible sign of the Church's inner struggle between holding up shining ideals and coping with tarnished reality. There are some people, for instance, who believe it is wrong to hand out condoms to young people, because it will 'encourage' them to have sex – like the mother who said 'children, don't put peas up your noses', thus planting in her offspring the immediate desire to do so. But if you don't give out the condoms, young people will surely go on having sex without them, merrily spreading preventable diseases that are far less acceptable than a little moral laxity.

People need rules to live by. The Catholic Church provides them. But as Christ so often showed, when you uphold the law for the law's sake, it can become a ball and chain. Christianity is about personal freedom. The Church seems to have got itself into a position where it distrusts the very freedoms it preaches. One former seminarian describes it as 'interposing itself between God and his people, to stop us making mistakes and going to hell'. Yet free will is fundamental to Christian doctrine, and the Church cannot lose faith in the free will of its members. 'There is an exaggerated fear that human nature will plan selfishly,' explains Bishop Murphy-O'Connor. 'The rules are trying to take away from that selfishness.'

Discussions around this thorny conflict surround the new Universal Catechism, currently being drawn up by the Vatican, in co-operation with bishops' conferences worldwide. Where the old-fashioned 'Penny Catechism' contained a final section of 'Thou Shalt Not' commandments, some church leaders are now recommending a more positive section of 'Thou Shalts'; a list of things which are blessed rather than blasted. How to climb to heaven, instead of how not to slither down the greasy pole to hell. (The Vatican, reports say, has yet to be convinced.)

Today's Christians are facing all kinds of urgent moral dilemmas – such as a yawning gulf between the rich west and the poor Third World. At least sex is clearly defined and reasonably quantifiable. Neatly categorised, from the venial sin (a rude thought) to the mortal (more or less everything else), there are few grey areas.

The more laws there are to break, the easier it is to become a criminal. Catholic sexual rules are a minefield, both for those who fail to keep them, and those who are supposed to enforce them. 'There are many other things in life – catastrophes – that the Church doesn't mention,' complains a university priest. 'For instance, I have never had anyone come to confession saying they have destroyed someone's character to the extent that the person has lost his or her job. Yet I would have thought this was more serious than a lot of the sexual things people come out with. There is a sense of the Church hammering on too much about sex.'

There is also a sense of the Church looking very silly in the process. Priests at parish level are only too aware of the foolishness of pushing *Humanae Vitae* as the party line, when many of their parishioners are happily ignoring it – and not even bothering to confess the fact. Confession is the traditional focus of the parish priest's power. He is the sponge who mops up the guilt, yet in order to keep his customers coming he must convince them that they need the service in the first place.

If sexual behaviour was wiped off the Church's agenda, the already dwindling queues outside the confessional would probably vanish altogether. Marco, an Italian brought up in London, is a regular communicant, but 'I haven't been to confession in twenty years,' he says. 'I wouldn't dream of it.'

When sex is a sin, absolutely everyone has something to confess, right down to little old ladies who have glimpsed a nipple on the television. Down the ages, the Church has ensured bums on pews by concentrating the burden of guilt on the sex lives of the faithful. Guilt – especially guilt connected with sexual 'impurity' – has been, up to now, an essential ingredient of the Catholic upbringing.

There's the joke about the Protestant who goes to hell. To his surprise, it's not bad – a hotel bar, with endless booze on tap. Then he looks out of the window, and sees tormented souls shrieking in a volcano of bubbling lava. So he says to the devil: 'I knew there had to be a catch somewhere.' But the devil replies: 'Don't worry, we just put that in for the Catholics. They insisted.'

The reality of Catholic sexual guilt is beyond a joke. Homosexuals, divorcees and the girlfriends of priests, for example, have to cope with an agonising burden of sin, and a sense that their Church has rejected them as worthless. In small Catholic communities, guilt and fear can breed hysterical malice. In 1984, a Kerry girl named Joanne Hayes broke down under pressure, and confessed to murdering a baby and dumping it in the sea. Forensic evidence did not support her culpability but who cared?[19] In the eyes of her neighbours, she was already a criminal, because she was an unmarried mother. The ruthless probing and condemning of Hayes's personal life enraged Irish feminists, and made the 'Kerry Babies' case a byword for narrow-minded Catholic prejudice. Her persecutors displayed a classic example of St Thomas Aquinas's 'holy hatred'.

Many of the Catholics we have spoken to have been victims of holy hatred, albeit less dramatically. There can be no doubt that the Vatican's inflexibility has caused untold grief and bitterness. Yet many others have been eager to stress the positive side of the Church – that in an age of uncertainty, it remains a strong, unchanging and ultimately benign structure, intimately concerned with the spiritual welfare of its members.

Nowadays, for the average Roman Catholic in Europe and America, there are two Churches. One is the Vatican, with its dessicated medieval morality. The other is their local parish church. Their experience of Roman Catholicism will largely depend on the character of their parish priest. It is he who attempts to bridge the painful, widening gap between the Church's ideals and social reality.

Imagine a young couple who are unable or unwilling to go along with the Church's ban of contraception. All they have to do is find a sympathetic priest (the more liberal clerics soon get a reputation) and explain their quandary. The kindly priest will then give them 'permission' to continue to receive the sacraments. It is a system that has obvious flaws. Michael, in his early twenties, found a trendy young Jesuit who was very sympathetic about what he saw as his besetting sin of masturbation. 'Unfortunately,' he says 'there came a day when I slipped into the usual confessional, confessed to wanking, and found he was on holiday. I was lectured severely by a miserable old sod of about eighty.'

The other flaw in the 'permission to be naughty' system is contained in the word permission. The trendiest, most liberal priest is still judging and controlling the sexual lives of his flock, in a way that few members of Protestant churches would tolerate for a moment. It cannot really be said to resolve that gulf between religious ideal and ordinary social practice. Among liberal Catholics, it is known as 'Black Market Morality'.

We would like to see a legislation of that black market. The heart of the argument against the Catholic Church's sexual rules is that they allow the Church an unacceptable degree of power, by setting standards and then deciding when, if ever, those standards may be relaxed. This book aims to strip away the accumulated layers of outdated morality, and find a way for Catholics to pursue sexual and romantic fulfilment. The argument currently raging in the Church is whether this way will take them further away from Christ or nearer.

Two: Childhood

> Maria struggled and tried to call for help, but she was being
> strangled, and could only protest hoarsely, gasping that she
> would be killed rather than submit. Whereupon Alexander
> half pulled her dress from her body and began striking at her
> blindly with a long dagger. She sank to the floor crying that
> she was being killed: Alexander plunged the dagger into her
> back and ran away.
>
> Life of St Maria Goretti, Virgin and Martyr
> Butler's *Lives of the Saints*[1]

'Today, if you're looking for Maria Goretti . . . try another galaxy,' writes the American Jesuit teacher, William J. O'Malley, in an article bewailing the 'cavalier treatment of sex' among modern teenagers.[2]

His regret seems odd when one considers the story of the Virgin and Martyr he holds up as an example to young people. Maria Goretti was a twelve-year-old Italian peasant girl, who died in 1902 of multiple stab-wounds after fending off an attempted rape. In her last hours, the child forgave her attacker and expired surrounded by a throng of admiring witnesses, including a priest, a Spanish noblewoman and two nuns. She was beatified in 1947, and canonised in 1950, while her repentant murderer was still living.

Her canonisation has some extremely peculiar, not to say unpleasant, implications. When Alexander decided to rape Maria, he was effectively presenting her with two choices. She could struggle and attain sainthood, with violent death as an unfortunate side-effect; or she could commit the sin of submitting to unlawful sexual intercourse, and survive as damaged goods. This dilemma is not confined to Catholic women – judges in rape trials are still inclined to count giving in to an attacker to avoid injury as a form of consent. But Maria's tragedy perfectly illustrates the Catholic Church's obsession with 'purity', the perfect state every child should strive for.

'Blessed are the pure in heart,' Christ said in his Sermon on the Mount, 'for they shall see God'.[3] It is a beautiful image, echoed by Rupert Brooke's line: 'this heart, all evil shed away, a pulse in the eternal mind, no less.'[4] However, the meaning the Church attaches to the concept of purity is far simpler. As Marina Warner writes: 'the way the educators of Catholic children have interpreted this for nearly two thousand years is sexual chastity.'[5] By canonising Maria Goretti, the victim of a hideous sexual crime, the Vatican was putting across the insidious message that a dead child is preferable to a raped one.

Most parents and teachers, of course, be they ever so staunchly Catholic, would strongly disagree. When it comes to the point, you won't find many people willing to tell a class of twelve-year-old girls to fight with an armed rapist. The ideal has little to do with reality, and an uncomfortable imbalance between the two runs through the whole of Catholic sexual morality like a bad drain. Which leads to the other implication of Maria's canonisation: that her example was valuable, because in her death, the idea and the reality – for once – came together. It was so rare. She fulfilled an ideal most young people would find impossible to live up to, and was therefore miraculous.

Teachers are left trying to bridge the gap between the reality of teenagers experimenting with sex, and the ideal (no sex whatever outside marriage) upheld by the Church. The sexual permissiveness of contemporary western society – the wide availability of contraception and dirty magazines stacked above the Liquorice Allsorts in every newsagents – makes the Church's rules seem ridiculously out of touch. Any Catholic teacher with half a notion of realism has, therefore, to go through mental contortions if they want to get the message across without sounding absurd.

There is encouraging evidence that, unlike Fr O'Malley, who would prefer to see all teenagers as fledgling Maria Gorettis, many teachers are rising to the challenge.

'We try to get away from the image that sex is riddled with guilt and sin,' says Ian Feely, Headmaster of a mixed Catholic comprehensive in Brighton. 'We can't overlook the fact that young men and women are maturing earlier these days. But we mustn't go to the other extreme of assuming that all young people are naturally promiscuous. As a Church school, we have to hold the high ground. We have to say, yes, it's fine to have relationships, and we understand that if you love the person, you might want to make love with them. We don't tell them relationships are wrong, but encourage them not to be promiscuous, not to cheapen sexuality. Of course we give them the counsel of perfection, the Church's line. But human beings are imperfect, and youngsters, in particular, need our help with the reality of their lives. We have to meet them where they are on their faith journey, or we'll lose them altogether.'

Mike Haywood, Head of Religious Education, agrees that achieving such a balance is no easy task. 'We don't have all the answers. Sexuality is a very important issue, and we have to be totally honest. It's no good talking exclusively about ideals if they're impossible to attain. We have to lose the image of the Pope as the one who says no to the pill – if the children see no relevance in what the Church has to offer them on relationships, they will most likely see no relevance in its teachings on social justice.'

And the Brighton school is not an isolated example. Catholic educators have had to address the issue of sexuality, whether they like it or not. The national curriculum in RE, set by a government unwilling to make Church schools a special case, means pupils must be equipped to answer exam questions about abortion, AIDS, drugs and homosexuality.

No wonder the hardliners, such as Fr O'Malley SJ, hanker for the good old days when black was black and white was white, and a 'delinquent' youth meant Micky Rooney in 'Boystown'. O'Malley and his fellow traditionalists are currently fighting a vigorous rearguard action against what they see as an invasive secular liberality, weakening the message of the Church. They argue that if children's sensibilities have been blunted by the permissive society, their teachers must simply turn up the volume.

O'Malley has a brisk method of dealing with the boys in his New York classes who tell him it's fine to have sex if the girl wants it too. 'The proper response, I think, is: "If somebody was willing to be your slave, would that make this particular slavery moral?"' He does not shrink from florid imagery. 'Youngsters literally gag,' he writes, 'when you suggest the possibility of bestiality. But if you don't know – or care – about your partner's hopes and dreams, what's the difference?'[6]

His fellow American, Fr Gerard S. Sloyan, is equally uncompromising. 'Catholic morality on sex can be summarised briefly: wait until marriage and then let your enjoyment of sex nourish your union, for children can come of it,' he writes, in a book intended for both young people and their teachers. 'This view of sex seems woefully outmoded in a culture that has separated sex from marriage almost entirely [. . .] Young Catholics need to hear early and often why their present happiness depends on total abstinence from sex before they marry.'[7]

Both Sloyan and O'Malley are priests of the old school, who firmly believe that keeping the faithful from sin is the sacred responsibility of anyone who wears a Roman collar. They are God's policemen, enforcing the inviolable laws laid down by the Vatican.

The question of who is more in tune with Rome's thinking on the subject – the Ian Feeleys of this world, or the Sloyans and O'Malleys – is a matter of some debate. The liberal camp would point to one of Vatican II's best-known encyclicals, *Gaudium et Spes*, which decreed that the sexual act is no longer sinful *per se*. In fact, under the right circumstances, it is even recognised as something apart from the procreation of children. 'Married love is uniquely expressed and perfected by the exercise of the acts proper to marriage,' declares this prim document. 'Hence the acts in marriage by which the intimate and chaste union of the spouses takes place are noble and honourable.'[8]

Gaudium hastens to add that sexual acts outside marriage are still extremely naughty, but by talking of a 'covenant of love' and recognising the sanctity of sex, it has made the job of teachers a little easier. The unfortunate fact remains, however, that a classroom full of adolescents is unlikely to be bowled over by a homily about the bond of marriage. One sixth-former at the Brighton comprehensive complains that 'sex is always talked about as if it was something only mums and dads do.'

And as we all know – though some of us would prefer not to – kids do it too. If they're not doing it, they're thinking about it. Early adolescence is the age at which sexual curiosity knows no bounds. We would not advocate chucking a handful of condoms into their midst and telling them to get on with it. In our view, adolescents are as hopeless at sex as they are at most other things. Leaving aside the possible emotional damage caused by teenage promiscuity, we hold to the old saying that sex is wasted on the young.

But the young disagree, as they always have and always will. Whether or not you approve, you have to deal with the unavoidability of that fact. It throws the more traditional teachers into an absolute lather. How do they guard the purity of the young minds in their care?

One method is to put them off with horror stories. A favourite old chestnut in Catholic schools is the emotive abortion film, *The Silent Scream*. This is a gory saga of dismembered foetuses and the 'killers' of these unborn children suffering the consequences of their actions. You do not have to be a rabid liberal to feel that this is a somewhat one-sided way to introduce a debate about the rights and wrongs of abortion. But of course, in Catholic-think, there is not, and never will be, another side. US Pro-Lifer Phyllis Schlafy remarks that 'It is very healthy for a young girl to be deterred from promiscuity by fear of contracting a painful, incurable disease, or cervical cancer, or sterility, or the likelihood of giving birth to a dead, blind or brain-damaged baby.'[9]

Two snags are apparent in this aversion-therapy. First, a child who sees images of sexual delight staring at her out of every advertisement is very unlikely to believe a word of it. Second, if the therapy does work, she will have trouble converting toxic sex into something 'noble and honourable' when she gets married. 'I was taught from an early age that marriage was a sacred institution, and that outside marriage I should never let a man near me,' says Pat, a fifty-one-year-old convent-educated Irish nurse. 'Consequently, I spent the whole of my teens and early twenties in complete fear of men and what they might do to me. I was so terrified of them, I couldn't even strike up an ordinary friendship. I now feel that this repression damaged me profoundly, and ruined my adolescence.'

Unsurprisingly, advocates of the horror-story method are few. Since Vatican II, the majority of Catholic teachers have, like Feely and Haywood, made genuine efforts to put across the Church's sexual rules with honesty, compassion and a healthy dose of realism. The mistakes of the past have been recognised at the highest level. One senior cardinal told us that 'in the past, it is undoubtedly true that mistaken emphases were placed in teaching about sex in schools, which were very damaging.'

The recognition – and indeed, the revolutionary effects of Vatican II on schools – has come too late for the likes of Pat. Catholics over the age of thirty, many of them parents of today's church-school pupils, recall only the *ancien régime*, in which they were lucky if they got any sex education at all. At Peter Stanford's school, run by the Christian Brothers, biology vanished from the curriculum after the examination of a fuchsia led to embarrassing questions about its connubial habits. Russian was substituted. Then, one momentous Thursday afternoon when he was sixteen, his class got their one and only lesson about sex. Most of the boys were baffled by what was being drawn on the blackboard, hardly recognising these illustrations as parts of their own bodies. Proceedings were halted by one boy rushing out to be sick at the mention of masturbation, and another fainting at the description of a vasectomy.

A colleague of Stanford's, who attended a small convent school, fared rather better. She managed to take biology A Level, but had to learn about human reproduction in secret, with the connivance of an enlightened nun.

Such stories spread back through generations of Catholic

schoolchildren. Frank Delaney, also educated by the Christian Brothers, in Ireland some twenty years earlier, recalls the fog of taboo which cloaked the process of procreation. 'In the USSR, it used to be said there was no religion. Well, in rural Ireland when I was growing up, there was no sex. All trace of anything carnal had to be removed. I did not know the accurate, vaginal facts of life until I was nineteen. I assumed it was rear entry, as I had seen among the animals. I thought all intercourse was anal. I was taught nothing. You had to rely on the instinct you felt when you saw a slightly raunchy photograph.'

There is a school of thought, by no means confined to Roman Catholics (and by no means abandoned – even our enlightened Brighton school could not bring itself to tell the kids about homosexuality), that drawing a veil over the whole area of human sexuality is the best way to bring up children, on the basis that what they don't know can't harm them:

> Yet ah! why should they know their fate?
>   Since sorrow never comes too late,
> And happiness too swiftly flies.
>   Thought would destroy their paradise.
> No more; where ignorance is bliss,
>   'Tis folly to be wise.[10]

Where sex is concerned, however, we feel ignorance is anything but blissful. Sexual ignorance destroys lives. Once upon a time, a fifteen-year-old schoolgirl, who had managed to conceal her 'shameful' pregnancy, gave birth in secret at a grotto dedicated to the Virgin Mary. The girl and her baby were both found dead the next morning.

This is not the outline of a nineteenth-century novel by the Abbé Prevost – it happened in Ireland, less than ten years ago. It is only too easy to give examples from that distressful country, because the Catholic sexual morality described by Frank Delaney remains enshrined in the country's constitution. Even in the north, where the British government has allowed greater freedoms, the 1967 Abortion Act has not yet hit the province's statute books.

The proposal to open a Brook Advisory Service in Belfast, in the autumn of 1991, caused a political storm and brought protesters onto the streets. Whitehall, which had given its backing to the plan, was soundly rapped on the knuckles by Catholic leaders. Bishop Patrick Walsh declared that giving teenagers advice about contraceptives would not allow them to lead moral lives.[11]

In August 1991, there was a storm in County Cork when a survey of teenage girls, carried out by the Northside Action Group in Cork City, criticised the 'frightening' level of sexual ignorance among young people, and blamed schools for spreading misinformation. A spokesperson for the group said that 'when asked about sex education, girls revealed that a nun had said in class they should not wear patent shoes because boys could see their private parts in the reflection, and that a teacher in another school told the girls that if they were sitting on a boy's lap they should put a paper between them for fear of getting pregnant.'[12]

Church leaders responded by branding the survey 'not scientific and not representative'. In September, the *Irish Catholic* printed the *pensées* of a Cork headmistress, Mrs Margaret Murphy; a classic proponent of the ignorance-is-bliss view. 'She points out that in countries where sex education has been available to children in school for many years the problems have escalated. Abortion figures have increased and moral values have degenerated, as young people experiment and use the information supplied to them.'[13]

In Ireland, the debate surrounding sex education is vigorous and often bitter. The Irish Catholic Church has yet to learn that declaring contraception and abortion illegal will not make them go away. *Cosmopolitan* magazine publishes a directory of charities and trusts which give abortion advice (both pro and anti). In the Irish edition, these pages are printed blank, but *Cosmopolitan*'s London office receives a steady stream of phone calls from Irish girls seeking help.

So using ignorance as a preventative measure is simply not good enough. And, as Frank Delaney observes: 'The human spirit will out.' At his school, it found an outlet in the mild smut of Harold Robbins' books, passed secretly from desk to desk. Michael Carson, author of the comic novel *Sucking Sherbet Lemons* did not need anything at all to stimulate his imagination. 'I knew I was peculiar before my teens,' he says. 'I used to have these dreams that I was lying naked on a platter, being eaten by our neighbours. It gave me an erotic thrill.' To each his own, but Carson significantly adds: 'There is no way not to corrupt children's minds. They'll find a way, if they've a disposition.'

The wise generation of post-Vatican II teachers will take this on board, and try to work round it. The old guard, however, feel their first duty lies in giving the means of purification. At a very early age, the traditionally brought-up Catholic child must learn the concept of shame.

Guilt and Shame

'Augustine,' says Marina Warner, 'is one of those pathways where history divides, and divides for the worse. St Augustine's doctrine of the inherent sinfulness of human flesh was presented at my convent school as a kind of silent prohibition. We were literally told to sleep with our hands on top of the coverlet. There was a great emphasis on the presence, the physical weight of the body, and the shame caused by its uncontrolled activities. I got into trouble because I had letters from boys. The nuns decided I had been "unchaste", and I was terribly attacked and punished. It upset me a lot.'

In his monumental work *City of God* St Augustine struggled to explain what he saw as the terrible problem of human sexuality. Clearly, he could not declare it absolutely wrong, because sexual intercourse was the method created by God for the reproduction of the species. And God definitely told Adam and Eve to 'be fruitful and multiply'.

But why was it surrounded by so much lust and wickedness? Surely that was not at all what God intended? Augustine worked out a complicated theory about reproduction before the Fall. If Adam and Eve had managed to remain in paradise, he explained, sex would have been entirely different – as God originally intended. 'Then (had there been no sin) the man would have sowed the seed and the woman would have conceived the child when their sexual organs had been aroused by the will, at the appropriate time and in the necessary degree, and had not been excited by lust.'[14]

In other words, sex in Eden was not enjoyable. Adam did not have to be aroused in order to get it up. There was no need for titillation or foreplay, because the sexual organs were under the control of his will. The lack of control associated with sex – the fact that the actions of the body seem to be independent of the mind and conscience – are a punishment for man's disobedience to God. Original sin – the fallout from Adam and Eve's crime – has left all of humankind with a fallen side to its nature. And that is sexuality.

'Man himself may have once received from his lower members an obedience which he lost by his own disobedience,' Augustine says, and he produces illustrations to give an idea of how this might have been. 'Some people can move their ears, either one at a time, or both together [. . .] There are others who imitate the cries of birds and beasts [. . .] A number of people produce at will such musical sounds from their behinds (without any stink) that they seem to be singing from that region.'[15]

So there you have it. In paradise, our father Adam could apparently fart the Posthorn Gallop, and order his willy to stand up, as easily as he wriggled his ears – ah, that lost world of bliss! And, what's more – 'the male seed could have been dispatched into the womb, with no loss of the wife's integrity, just as the menstrual flux can now be produced from the womb of a virgin without loss of maidenhood.'[16] Don't ask how – with God, all things are possible.

After the Fall, man became possessed by lust, beyond all reason. His genitals were out of his own control, and the mere

sight of anything female filled him with wicked desires, unconnected with the procreation of children. 'It is right, therefore, to
be ashamed of lust, and it is right that the members which it
moves [. . .] should be called "pudenda" [parts of shame], which
they were not called before man's sin.'[17]

Augustine's fear and loathing of women and their sexuality
would be laughable, if it had not been enshrined in Catholic
morality and hence in Church schools. He did not like women, he
did not even enjoy their company. Unfortunately, his unruly
body disagreed. There was nothing for it but to avoid the sight of
women altogether – lust was always her fault.

This is the realisation that has traditionally hit Catholic children like a hammer-blow at the onset of puberty, and before.
Boys suffer the shame of uncontrollable genitals. Girls bear the
'curse' of menstruation, and the sole responsibility for leading
boys into sin. 'It goes back to the idea that a woman's identity is
totally bound up in her body,' says Marina Warner, 'so that the
actions of her body – even unwilled – are sinful. Even if she is
raped, she has committed a sin, which is the most extraordinary
moral thinking. I was certainly taught that sex is a much greater
crime for a woman.'

Over the centuries, these ideas have bled into society at large. It
is not only Catholic girls who feel they have committed some
unknown, unwilled crime in acquiring the body of an adult
female. But Catholic children have the added fear of sin, and the
awareness of sexual sin can be drummed into them at a very early
age.

'It leads, I think,' says Warner, 'to the sexualisation of children.
One of the effects of the traditional Catholic upbringing is that
you are carnal before you're even conscious – all that stuff about
keeping your skirt down and your legs together.' This teaching,
like so much else, is gradually changing in western Catholicism.
But it has left its mark on generations of people.

You are never too young to commit a sexual sin, the theory
goes. An otherwise sensible Anglican woman told us, in all
seriousness, that the time-honoured C. of E. tradition of pederas-
tic Scout Masters occurred because their Boy Scouts 'led them

on'. No, you don't have to be a Catholic for this one either. But it obviously helps.

'There were about five of us girls, aged ten, in a Catholic Primary School,' remembers Brenda, now twenty-nine. 'We were lying in the sun, trying to sunbathe. So we drew our skirts up. And a teacher told us off for deliberately provoking the boys. I had absolutely no idea what she was talking about. We were ten years old, and she was telling us off for being wanton women!'

Daniella, a Maltese in her early fifties, says her teenage years were dominated by the feeling that anything to do with her body was sinful. 'I remember being told off for wearing lipstick, because it made my mouth look like "a lump of raw meat", whilst at the same time being encouraged to look beautiful, because my body was the temple of the Holy Spirit. I was never quite sure where the line between being beautiful and being sexy lay.'

Sandra, forty-two, brought up in an Italian community in London, was nearly expelled from her convent school for wantonness during a retreat. 'I did a drawing of a pregnant, nude woman, hidden under a holy book. When Mother Evelina saw it, her lips went bright red, she was so angry. I was taken to the head, Mother Ambrosia (another tight-lipped nun – the nice ones always had thick lips) and she told me I was wicked and would end up in Borstal.'

The teachers of these young limbs of Satan were working on the assumption that man's natural state is one of boiling lust. Some would go to blush-making lengths to ensure that the minds of their charges were unsmirched by naughty thoughts. In order to do this, they had to invade what the Bible describes as the 'moist places' of the mind, and most Catholics over thirty can recall humiliating violations of their privacy.

'Whether or not you knew something was sinful,' says Frank Delaney, 'the priest asked you anyway, when you went to confession. "Did you have any sins of the body, my child?" I had to ask what they were.'

Mark, a twenty-nine-year-old journalist educated at an expensive Benedictine boarding school, remembered the 'laundry-list attitude' to sexuality in the confessional. 'It was, have you committed self-abuse, and if so, how many times? The monks fell into two categories. First, the sort who were totally embarrassed about the whole thing – you knew they were embarrassed, so you just wrote them off as idiots. Second, there was the sort who were much more interested than they should have been in little boys' sex lives.'

Nosy priests and nuns know perfectly well that no matter how you keep the sexes apart, or try to fill children's ears with horror stories, there is at least one kind of adolescent sexual activity you cannot prevent.

If your hand or your foot should be your downfall, cut it off

Matt 18: 8

Masturbation is, for most people, the introduction to their sexuality. Down the ages, this cheap, safe and agreeable pastime has been surrounded with a hysterical fear which, we believe, must be because it is done purely for pleasure, without the least possibility of increasing the human race.

In the last century, children were told that masturbation caused blindness, tuberculosis and a softening of the bones. Young women with nervous disorders were forced to admit they had been masturbating and 'cured' by removal of their clitorises.

British boys' public schools formed elaborate rules to obliterate 'beastliness', including dormitory patrols, sewing up trouser pockets, exhausting organised games and compulsory cold showers – Spartan conditions were supposed to lower the sex drive. The death of Dean Frederick Farrar's Victorian schoolboy hero, in his cautionary novel *Eric, or Little by Little*, was caused by beastliness.

Nowadays, masturbation is still a taboo – few people boast to their mates in the pub about the fantastic wank they had last night. It is, however, generally recognised to be harmless, and the parents who fill their children with guilt by insisting it is dirty are in the minority. In Catholic schools and parishes, if mentioned at all, it tends to be dealt with in a relaxed and liberal fashion. But today's liberal teachers should be warned, officially, it is still a grave sin. Here is the latest piece of Vatican wisdom on wanking, dating from 1975:

> The traditional Catholic doctrine that masturbation constitutes a grave moral disorder is often called into doubt or expressly denied today. It is said that psychology and sociology show that it is a normal phenomenon of sexual development, especially among the young. It is stated that there is real and serious fault only in the measure that the subject deliberately indulges in solitary pleasure closed in on self, because in this case the act would indeed be radically opposed to the loving communion between persons of different sex, which some hold is what is principally sought in the use of the sexual faculty.
>
> This opinion is contradictory to the teaching and pastoral practice of the Catholic Church. [. . .] both the Magisterium of the Church [. . .] and the moral sense of the faithful have declared without hesitation that masturbation is an intrinsically and seriously disordered act. [. . .] Even if it cannot be proved that Scripture condemns this sin by name, the tradition of the Church has rightly understood it to be condemned in the New Testament when the latter speaks of 'impurity', 'unchasteness' and other vices contrary to chastity.[18]

In our view, one of the most significant things about the above statement is the open admission that the 'tradition' of the Church is more important than the Scriptures. The older, unreconstructed branches of the Vatican, at the top of the Catholic tree, very clearly regret that Christ and St Paul said so little about sex, but claim to know what they thought. It can't be said too often – if all the Catholic sexual rules had undisputed Biblical backup, the New Testament would be as long as the London Telephone Directory.

The 'tradition' that masturbation is a mortal sin (a sin that separates a person from God) has caused deep and we believe unnecessary misery to generations of young Catholics, and it continues to be an obstacle in the path of childless couples wishing to have fertility treatment. One of the Vatican's objections to *in vitro* fertilisation is that the man's semen has to be produced by masturbation.

Rock star turned charity worker Bob Geldof gives a vivid account of his adolescent guilt in his autobiography, *Is That It?* 'Masturbation had become part of my daily life. And not just daily. It was a mortal sin, of course. At school during retreats one of the priests would go on about it. Your body was the temple of the Holy Ghost, and if you abused it, you abused God, because the Holy Ghost was in God. It was throwing your seed on fallow ground. You would tell that in confession to get rid of the sin, but when they told you to stop, you knew you couldn't.'[19]

In Mark's Benedictine boarding school, in the late 1970s, the subject was kept at an embarrassed distance. 'The monks were all very nice, but they had absolutely no idea about sex,' he says. 'I mean, they knew we masturbated, but they couldn't handle the circumstances that led to masturbation – porn mags, or an interest in the matron's tits. All they had to fall back on was their theological teaching.'

And, one might add, their prejudice against women. Keep females out of the way, lest they become 'occasions of sin' – that still seems to be the rule in Catholic boarding schools. One of the poshest was rocked by a scandal a couple of years ago when one of the junior matrons was found to be pregnant. She had been having relationships with more than one pupil. When the father was traced, he was given a sharp slap on the wrist. The woman was sacked.

Mark argues that all-male environments are unhealthy and that masturbation is only the most obvious side-effect. 'We were cut off from female influence. There were some daughters of masters, but that stopped quickly, after a pregnancy scare with one of them. The only sexual education we had were talks from crusty old monks who knew nothing about relationships with women. We relied on a surfeit of pornographic magazines of every description – really, the only thing was your right hand and a magazine.'

Dirty magazines are not the ideal introduction to the opposite sex. Mark admits that his school experiences had a profound – and not always positive – effect on his sexual attitudes. He does not, however, entirely reject his education. 'I think that with all Church rules on sexuality, there is a core of truth you cannot do away with. I think excessive masturbation, for instance, is terrible. I know it has done me a lot of damage. Sex is really meant for expression with another person. It's a covenant of love.'

Catholics educated during the last twenty years will often express similarly qualified approval of the Church's sexual teachings. Sexual morality is not, in itself, a bad thing. Ignoring everything the Church has to say on the subject would be throwing the baby out with the bathwater. Even the notorious *Humanae Vitae* is felt to have its points. 'It's beautifully written,' Mark says, 'and the core of it, what it says about marriage and relationships and the values we must place on life, is very important. Unfortunately, they put the ruling about the pill in the middle of it.'

A rising generation of Roman Catholics is (in defiance of the mustier elements in the Vatican) making up its own mind about which rules it wishes to keep and which should be crossed out of the book.

The Future

Today's Catholic schoolchildren were born into a Church that hovers uneasily between extremes of conservatism and liberalism; an upheaval that is itself a symptom of dramatic change. What kind of sexual morality will they bring to the Church of the next century?

The sixth-formers we spoke to at the mixed Brighton comprehensive treated the Church's moral teachings with affectionate scepticism – their attitude to sexual sin was relaxed and without fear. Asked if they agreed with *Humanae Vitae*, they laughed. 'But if you are allowed to argue in class with the Church's teachings,' one girl said, 'then you don't resent it.'

'It's no good just arguing to be awkward, though,' one of the boys shrewdly pointed out. 'You have to have good reasons, because the Church's rules are there, and they won't budge.'

One of the girls complained that sex in the school curriculum was muffled in too much flannel. 'There's a lot of talk about it. But it's like the point at the centre of the circle, and we're always going round and round it, without actually getting anywhere.'

Her friend displayed a more combative attitude. 'It's no good the Church telling me what to do on abortion if I'm not allowed to use contraception.' Young priests were popular with these sixth-formers, but older ones were seen as people who might tell on them to their parents. 'There was one who kept pressing me about what I did at parties. I didn't know at the time what he wanted me to say.'

The general consensus, however, was that their Catholic teaching gave them sensible guidelines, rather than restrictions. 'This school is more caring, more friendly, because it is Catholic. The teachers don't just see it as a job. Friends who don't go to Catholic schools see sex as without responsibility. We know about the responsibilities.'

What they did not know about was the traditional Catholic guilt of their parents' generation. Their experience of Church dominated education had been liberal and positive. The girls were puzzled by an explanation of the female temptress role, so much a feature of old-fashioned Catholic education. All felt there were certain cases in which abortion could be justified.

The fifth- and sixth-form boys at an expensive Benedictine public school were more critical of their education. 'The contraception question was dealt with in forty minutes,' complained one, 'and only because it was on the exam syllabus. The discussions are always from a certain point of view. You're directed. The monks can only tell us not to do things they know we're doing already.'

'The sex education here isn't relevant to our generation,' another stated. 'The Church needs a Vatican III. I think, generally, sex is equated with badness.'

The all-male environment was felt to damage their attitudes to girls. 'Girls would get stressed if they were in our biology class,' piped up one little horror in the fifth form, 'because some boys say that a woman's place is in the home.'

'Catholicism is afraid of sex,' declared a boy in the lower sixth. 'When I go on holiday I meet girls, and if I can go all the way, I will. I can't wait to get to university.' This one has evidently swallowed the old-fashioned Catholic notion that the whole world outside the Church is a sink of licentiousness. One hopes he won't be disappointed.

We found a flavour of the *ancien régime* in the way this public school was run. Although the emphasis in RE is on discussing and weighing up different moral stances, the Church's included, many of the boys felt that the monks refused to treat them as moral beings. 'It's no good teaching us to make the right choices, if they then won't trust us with girls,' one pointed out.

The boys described the regular sixth-form dances, held with local girls' schools under careful supervision. The fifth-formers, bless 'em, were looking forward to this contact with the opposite sex with bated breath. But their more jaded elders pointed out that being patrolled by the monks ruled out even the most innocent thrills. The lack of trust shown in them was felt to be an insult.

Asked what they would take away with them after their schooling, the pupils did generally find something positive to say. 'This is better than a school with no morality,' one said. 'At the core of it are the basic choices of right and wrong.'

What these boys shared with the pupils of the mixed comprehensive, however, was a feeling that the teachings of the Church would not be of much use in their future lives. The guilt and fear surrounding sexuality may have been jettisoned by a new generation of teachers, but their success in getting over any clear, distinct message – holding the middle ground, as Ian Feely puts it – must be open to question. Many of today's Catholic parents, however, far from disapproving of their children's relaxed attitude to sex, see it as something to celebrate.

'I envy my kids for the relaxed and sensible attitude they have to sex,' one Catholic mother told us. 'They have none of my hang-ups, and I think it can only make them better people.' But for every mother like this, there is one like the well-known moralist and mother of ten, Victoria Gillick, who wants to keep adolescents and contraception surgically separated. The traditional Catholic rulings on sexuality are dying hard and painfully.

For, of course, it is not only schoolteachers who shape the attitudes of teenagers. Parents remain the first and usually decisive influence. Sally, a solicitor in her twenties, went to a 'not too regressive' convent school, but received a handsome legacy of sexual hang-ups from her mother. 'She is an Italian Catholic from a little island where, even now, if you go out with someone for a short time, you can't then marry anyone else. You become "used goods".'

Through her mother, Sally developed an obsession with the sinfulness of sex that her schooling did nothing to change. 'As a code of morals, it is quite hard to get rid of, because it defines how you see yourself, and presents you with an image of what you should be as a female. If you grow up with that, you can't just decide one day to chuck it out of the window. So many other parts of you are tied up with it.'

As Philip Larkin would say. 'They fuck you up, your mum and dad/ They may not mean to, but they do.'[20] All the more reason, then, for sex education which will equip young people for real, loving relationships in the real world. Most of today's Catholic teachers do their best to show a Church founded and run on love, rather than repression.

But a cloak of liberality and a free use of trendy buzzwords such as 'openness' and 'honesty' cannot disguise the bald fact of the Church's official teaching. The Church remains committed to a rigorous and negative sexual morality, that no amount of caring flannel can disguise.

'At this age,' writes RE teacher Daniel Corey in his book,

The Family, widely used for sex education in Catholic schools, 'you should be aware that religious and moral answers are not absolute proofs. They are not like the answers you give to a mathematical problem.'[21]

The tone of Corey's book is jokey, relaxed and modishly touchy-feely. But scratch the surface, and you're back to square one: 'Question: What would be the dangers to society and children if it were acceptable to have sexual intercourse with anyone at any time?'[22]

The current fashion for concentrating on the 'wonderfulness' of sex is not a sign of true progress. The Catholic Church still works from the assumption that sexual intercourse is as dangerous as an addictive drug. Just as heroin is 'wonderful' for cardiac infarctions or terminal cancers, but not to be touched under any other circumstances, the sexual act is only wonderful within marriage.

Three:
Years of Indiscretion

'I started to doubt about the age of fifteen. It was around the question, entirely theoretical at the time, of the Church's teaching on contraception.'

Clare Short MP[1]

'My chief difficulties about the Church centre around her attitude to sex. So a case could evidently be made out for the Church being an alternative to sexual life. Whatever the truth is, it is certainly a fact in my own life that I have always had an either/or attitude about sex and the spiritual life.'

Antonia White[2]

'The Church is a conduit to AIDS, in that the only option it gives gay people is perpetual celibacy or perpetual promiscuity.'

Fr Bernard Lynch

'From the World, the Flesh and the Devil,' cries the Church of England's *Book of Common Prayer*, 'Good Lord Deliver us!' World, flesh and devil have always operated as an inseparable three-some in the Christian mind, like a firm of solicitors. To become a young adult, distanced from the influences of home, Church and school, means entering the world and getting acquainted with the devilish temptations of the flesh.

Most people spend their early twenties discovering their sexuality, and probably experiencing their first close relationships. It is a fact of modern life, much deplored by the Church, that the majority of young adults feel they have a right to sex without strings. This means, of course, using contraception. And, because stringless sex is wholly at odds with Church teaching, the young Catholic adult often feels that he or she is faced with a straight choice between the world and the Church. Guess which one is winning.

A 1991 survey in the Italian magazine *Jesus* showed that while 98 per cent of Italian children are baptised, less than half keep the faith into adult life.[3] Despite the best efforts of parishes and schools, there is a chronic shortage of young bums on pews. The typical congregation has a preponderance of small children and very old people. There is a fine old Catholic tradition of hobbling back to Church when you are too ancient and toothless to commit any more sins of the flesh. The implication is that the demands of the Catholic life are fine for Grandma and the kids, but impractical for anyone in between.

It is an old problem and the Church has always made frantic efforts to woo these young apostates back into the fold. It has also been quick to sling blame back at World, Flesh & Devil, Ltd. For example, many a pulpit diatribe has been directed against the 'false gods' of communism and socialism for luring the young away from the Church. During the Spanish Civil War, the Catholic Church's support of Franco against the socialists was notorious – only a few priests and religious orders worldwide dared to condemn the fascist dicator.

Since the 1960s, however, the Liberation Theology of South America has blended radical politics with religion, infusing controversy and vitality in equal measure. Pope John Paul II has preached against capitalism and materialism as incompatible with the message of Christ. Modern Catholicism is right-on. It is the social teaching of the Catholic Church that has, in this century, given rise to organisations such as Young Christian Workers – early stamping ground of the politicians Jacques Delors and Chris Patten. The YCWs continue to inspire many, with their inner city missions and 'option for the poor' in the Third World.

But highlighting the powerful social teaching (often dubbed 'the Church's best-kept secret') has not stopped young adults turning their backs on the Church. Their reasons for lapsing are usually fairly prosaic, having more to do with little bits of stretchy rubber than ideology. Only 22 per cent of those interviewed for the survey in *Jesus* magazine agreed that sex outside marriage was wrong. Only 36 per cent agreed with the Church that homosexuality was 'intrinsically disordered'.[4]

Dr Michael Hornsby-Smith's survey of English parish opinion revealed that two thirds of the official advisers to the English bishops reject the papal teaching on contraception.[5] 40 per cent of those questioned felt that a woman would be justified in having an abortion under certain circumstances – despite the fact that defence of the unborn child has become the cornerstone of orthodoxy in many western Catholic churches.

Such figures should be setting off alarm bells in the corridors of the Vatican. Its authority in matters sexual is crumbling fast – has already crumbled, some would say. But the disturbing evidence tends to be received with martyr-like murmurs about the unpopularity of true prophets. Collectively, the Church knows it is right. Anyone who disagrees with it is wrong. No notion of reconsidering the teaching on sex is even entertained.

The latest scapegoat for the growing eclipse of the Church's influence is the media. Valerie Riches, of the Responsible Society, speaks for many when she complains that young people are hypnotised by the magical powers of the media into having sex before marriage. 'Most significant is the message that comes from the pop culture and teenage magazines. With honourable exceptions, these promote the idea that sexual activity among young people outside marriage is acceptable, provided contraceptives are used. More and more contraceptive propaganda aimed at the young has simply meant more abortions.'[6]

Because this statement so perfectly reflects the traditionalist Catholic view, it is worth looking into the implications behind it. Firstly, is sexual activity outside marriage acceptable? Unlike Mrs Riches, the authors believe there are degrees of acceptability. For instance, we would not encourage promiscuity in teenagers because of the proven health risks and possible psychological damage. But what about responsible young adults, involved in longer relationships which might not lead to marriage? We find that acceptable in itself, and we find the use of contraception even more so. The paranoiac phrase 'contraceptive propaganda' suggests a malign plot to get a condom on every willy, simply for its own sake. We feel that 'information' is a more suitable word than 'propaganda' in this context. If people must have sex outside marriage – and these days, they obviously do – contraception is imperative.

Abortion

The debate surrounding abortion has little to do with this book. Obviously abortions are the result of two people having sex. But as soon as conception has occurred, the issue ceases to be about sex, and centres around the sanctity of human life. The Catholic Church, holding human life to be sacred from the moment of conception, is implacably opposed to abortion.

When a couple find themselves with an unwanted pregnancy, they must decide whether they consider the cluster of cells inside the woman to be a human life, with rights equal to those of its mother. If they don't, an abortion is a surgical operation. If they do, they must examine the morality of destroying that life. Neither issue falls under the heading of this book.

The Church, in its continuing campaign of sexual pessimism, stubbornly links the abortion question with sex. It believes in something it calls the 'contraceptive mentality'. Women who get used to taking the pill, goes the argument, have already decided that if the pill fails, they will automatically opt for an abortion.

We believe this view insults women. We have never met anyone who had an abortion for fun. We maintain that women – particularly Catholic women – take contraceptive precautions in order to avoid facing this situation. The Church has a powerful and laudable reverence for human life. Its great mistake is attaching the same amount of sin-value to two entirely different acts – preventing conception and terminating a pregnancy. The logic here is deeply flawed. If abortion is so terrible, all the more reason to make contraceptives widely available and morally acceptable, so that fewer abortions will be necessary in the first place.

By continuing to vilify those who have abortions, we believe that the Catholic Church undermines its own message of Christian compassion and respect for human life. In recent years, young girls going into abortion clinics have been harrassed and abused by screaming crowds of pro-life demonstrators. We have been disgusted to observe wearers of Roman collars among these crowds. 'If Jesus was around today,' remarks Andrew Maggs, a young seminarian, 'he would not be protesting outside abortion clinics and abusing women going in. He would be at the back door, giving them a helping hand when they leave.'

The arguments against abortion go right back to the roots of Catholic doctrine. In 'City of God', St Augustine set his face against 'depraved married persons' who use poisons to 'stifle within the womb and eject the foetus that has been conceived'. Such people, says Augustine, 'do not deserve the name of husband and wife . . . it was not for wedlock but for fornication that they became united . . . either the woman is the mere mistress of the husband, or the man is the paramour of the wife.' Observe how rapidly Augustine boils the issue down to the sin of the sexual act. He dwells upon this far more than the human rights of the foetus.

In its 1974 Declaration on Procured Abortion, the Vatican reinforced Augustine's linking of abortion to the sin of wishing for sexual pleasure for its own sake. It suggests that men and women who consider themselves free to 'seek sexual pleasure to the point of satiety, without taking into account any law or the essential orientation of sexual life towards fertility' would scarcely think twice about their 'right to dispose of human life'.

In the late 1970s, an Italian nun told a classroom full of schoolgirls: 'Some of you will marry and have loving husbands and children. And some of you will have abortions.' Abortions, in the mind of this woman, were a direct result of ignoring the Church's teachings about sex.

Feminists within the Church have also identified the usual strain of misogyny; the wish to keep women prisoners of their biology. It is the woman who carries the burden of sin for an abortion, whatever the reasons and whatever the attitude of the foetus' father. Her life and health fade into insignificance. She becomes a mere vessel for the cells she is carrying. 'I think that human life is too valuable and precious a thing to be created when one is unable to bring it into this world,' says Frances Kissling, president of the US organisation Catholics for a Free Choice. 'As someone who believes in the dignity of women, I respect myself too much to place myself in a situation where I create a life that I am unable or unwilling to nurture.'

By forbidding contraception, the Church is very possibly increasing the number of abortions. The authors have personal reservations (entirely unconnected with sexual morality) about abortion. But we consider contraception and abortion to be two separate issues.

Punishment Built In

Let us suppose, for the sake of argument, that contraception always works. What is the real problem, then? That it isolates the purely pleasurable side of sex. We're back with the old, underlying Christian assumption that sex itself is wicked and wrong, unless you are heterosexual, married and intending to produce children.

Many young Catholics feel that this assumption, drummed into them from an early age, makes them totally unfitted for relationships and – paradoxically – more instead of less likely to come to grief. Catholic guilt is not always strong enough to prevent a young person from having sex. But it can be strong enough to surround the act with anguish and confusion.

'I used to go out with a boy who, when he heard I was Catholic, said "Oh, no!",' recalls twenty-nine-year-old Brenda. 'Before me, he'd gone out with another Catholic girl who was so guilty about sex that before orgasm she'd pretend to faint, and then say afterwards "What happened?" She wanted to be absolved from any conscious decision. That's why I think Catholic girls get pregnant more often. Even if they could get the pill, they don't want to make a conscious decision about doing it, because that's far worse than just throwing caution to the winds.'

Wendy Perriam, whose novels explore the Catholic relationship with sex, agrees. She believes that entering adulthood stamped with the letters RC, like a stick of seaside rock, has wrought havoc in her emotional life. 'I was told that if I made love to someone not my husband, I would go to hell immediately. Whenever I did it, I still half believed that I would be damned to hell for all eternity. For years, it never crossed my mind that I should get any pleasure from sex. I didn't use contraception for ages, because I didn't want to compound the sin of sex. I had been brought up with the Catechism: "What must I do when I go to bed? . . . compose myself modestly, and go to sleep with my last thoughts on my crucified saviour." It makes going to bed with a man bloody difficult.'

Perriam believes that Catholicism also affects romantic choices. 'I think that being brought up as a Catholic gives you a taste for sexual masochism. You are drawn to men like the Catholic God – strict, judgemental and punishing. If you have horrible sex, when you're hurt, you get the punishment built in.'

As we saw in the previous chapter, the modern Church has gone a long way towards changing its sexual teaching, making a serious attempt to cast out the terror felt by those of Perriam's generation. But the notion of compromise has yet to reach the pinnacle of the hierarchy. John Paul II, the charismatic Polish pontiff who champions the poor and pleads for Third World debts to be written off, remains so smitten with the anti-sex message of *Humanae Vitae* that he is reported to have written a new encyclical to enforce it.

The fact that the world has not yet seen this is due to certain pragmatic advisers – notably the Norman Tebbit of the Holy See, the German Cardinal Joseph Ratzinger, than whom no *éminence* could be more *grise*. With a shrewd eye to public image, the Cardinal is said to have persuaded the Pope to hold his fire for the time being. He appears to feel that while the Church cannot go back on *Humanae Vitae*, there is no mileage in pushing it. The vast majority of western priests are seldom heard preaching its virtues (though they do sometimes lapse into eulogies about Vatican-approved 'natural' family planning). And they report that in the confessional, taking the pill rarely features in the litany of penitents' sins. So all in all, why go out of the way to aggravate an old sore?

We have seen that today's young Catholics are emerging from their schools with a clear idea of the Church's teaching on sexual morality, but also with an idea of what is right for them. The two are rarely compatible and, all too often, the Church is the loser.

Possibly, this generation will be the first to feel free to make its own sexual choices and to stay within the Church. In his survey, Dr Hornsby-Smith spoke of the emergence of a 'customary Catholicism', based on the received teachings of the Church, but tailored by society's mores to fit individual requirements.[7] Some hardliners dismiss this as à la carte Christianity and hold to the old adage that if you can't stand the heat you should get out of the kitchen.

At grass-roots level – a long way from the Vatican – pragmatism appears to be winning the day. If this keeps the young within the fold, even when they decide to go their own way with sex, then the unhappy experiences of earlier generations may not be repeated. For them, it was all or nothing. If they strayed from the path of righteousness and had sex before marriage, they either felt so racked with guilt that they could never enjoy it or they left the Church altogether, believing it had no place for them.

Sandra, now divorced, feels her Italian-Catholic upbringing in London has a lot to answer for. She left her convent school with little idea of how pregnancy occurs, and paid dearly for her ignorance. 'I never knew when my fertile periods were. When I asked my form teacher at the convent, she said to ask the priest.

After school, I went to work at a hotel in Italy, and took a shine to Stephano. It was his aunt's hotel. When she found out I was pregnant, I got the sack. I tried to have a back street abortion in Italy, but the woman said it would go wrong.'

Sandra returned to London and went through the pregnancy with the support of her parents. She married Stephano – reluctantly – because it was 'the right thing to do'. She felt rejected by the Church. 'The day before the wedding I went to confession, to this American priest. He said I was wicked and that I didn't deserve to marry. I was so upset that I fainted during the wedding service.'

The marriage was not a happy one. Sandra felt she had been betrayed by the Church, but did not entirely move away from it. Religious belief does not vanish simply because it is inconvenient. The Catholics who suffer most acutely from the Church's sexual morality are those, like Sandra, who fall foul of the rules but cannot bear to leave the fold. 'I went away from the institution,' she says, 'but it didn't stop me loving God. There were times when I used to say to him "When will you stop punishing me for being bad?" But I decided it was my cross and I had to get on with it.'

Once a Catholic, the old saying goes, always a Catholic. The pull of the Church can be as mild as G. K. Chesterton's 'twitch upon the thread',[8] or as powerful as Thompson's slavering Hound of Heaven. Sandra is angry with the Church, because she feels it turned its face from her when she needed it, and condemned her when she was suffering. She is currently being wooed back, but for every Sandra there are countless other young Catholics who make efforts to sever the thread altogether. The strain put upon them by the granite inflexibility of the Church's sexual rules is just too much to bear.

Cutting the Cord

> Today, there are many who vindicate the right to sexual
> union before marriage . . . this opinion is contrary to
> Christian doctrine, which states that every genital act must be
> within the framework of marriage.
>
> *Declaration on Certain Questions Concerning Sexual Ethics*, 1975

The choice is a simple one – marriage and 'genital acts' or the single, sexless life. The formal language used by Rome always manages to give the impression that the leaders of the Church wish we could take our genitals off and lock them up until wanted. 'Experience teaches us,' continues the document quoted above, 'that love must find its safeguard in the stability of marriage.'

Never mind that divorce rates are soaring. For a Catholic, marriage lasts forever, therefore it is stable. And paradoxically, it is the binding nature of Catholic marriage that makes young RCs so wary about doing it. What 'experience' can possibly have taught a conference of celibate bishops about marriage, heaven alone knows. 'Experience' should also have shown them that modern young people, in the process of learning about their own sexuality, will not wait until marriage to have sex.

They are all too likely to decide that where sex is concerned, it's a case of World one, Church nil. When Brenda emerged from her convent school into the sixth form of a mixed comprehensive, she was 'overwhelmed' to discover that the other girls were doing it and talking about it. 'I remember saying to one girl, who was sleeping with her boyfriend, "I can't believe you're so crass about it – you talk about it as if it was a good exercise, like swimming!" And she said: "But it is." Well, the idea that it was a healthy pastime was certainly new to me.' In the face of such peer pressure, do you join them or beat them?

For Mark, the Benedictine-educated journalist, the choice was agonising. 'I was consumed with guilt,' he says. 'Before going to bed with my girlfriend – who became my wife – I used to go and

60

puke. It's part of my make-up to be nervous, to worry excessively about things. And the Catholic view of sex exacerbated that.'

Sally, in her early twenties, tried shutting out the temptations of the world by throwing herself totally into Catholicism. 'I took it on very seriously for a while, but the strain was unbearable. The demands they make were beyond me. And it wasn't only sex. There were other things that seemed much harder. I always felt, for example, that you should give up most of your money. But no one else seemed to take that part very seriously. In the end, I grew to resent it. I now feel only hostility.'

The experience of breaking with the Church over sex in the late teens and early twenties is a common one. Stephen, Liverpool-born, claims that his Catholic upbringing has left him with a curious, verbal form of premature ejaculation – he has a compulsion to blurt out 'I love you' to any woman he sleeps with, so he can persuade himself that he is not having 'casual' sex.

He recalls going to mass after he had lost his virginity. 'I was convinced that the crucifix was staring at me. Each time I looked up, I felt Jesus' eyes burning into me. It was as if he was determined to tell everybody what I had done. I couldn't take communion. But when I stayed in the pew while the others trooped up to the altar, I felt as if everybody in the church must be able to imagine what I had been up to. I persevered with mass for a while, but it was so painful that very soon it started being every other week, then once a month, until now it's only when I go home to my parents.'

Virgins for the Kingdom

As an alternative to peer group pressure, the Church encourages organisations for young people, which – consciously or not – harness burgeoning adolescent energy and channel it into worthy, sexless zones. A restless young person may join his or her local parish youth group (entrance 50p, leave your hormones at the door). At diocesan level, they can volunteer as a care attendant for disabled people making pilgrimage to Lourdes, or link up with various community schemes.

James, a writer now in his twenties was offered a variety of caring activities as a sixth-former at a private school run by the Christian Brothers. These were often undertaken in conjunction with the girls from the local convent. 'There was visiting the elderly, fund-raising for the St Vincent de Paul Society, a club that the sixth-formers ran for the mentally handicapped once a week.'

And all these activities centred on a thriving charismatic prayer group. 'It was all strumming guitars, singing very simple but very rousing charismatic hymns, praising the Lord and getting very emotional. At that age, you are so pained and self-conscious. The charismatic prayer-group was a way of letting go. Other boys in the school who didn't get involved called us the God Squad and, in a way, I think I was proud of that tag.'

Young people are torn between the desire to establish their own identities, and the desire to run with the pack. The charismatic movement – feared and mistrusted by many elements in the Christian Churches – has proved a magnet for youth. Spreading across all shades of Christian thought, it is based upon the idea of a fervently emotional, deeply personal individual relationship with God. This individualism is balanced by services which, some say, work up to a pitch of mass hysteria. The sex drive is sublimated into worship.

In such an environment, the temptations of the world and the flesh can be kept at a safe distance. 'I remember I always looked forward to the kiss of peace,' says James. 'It made touching girls OK because it was all done in a religious context. It made me feel very grown up because I could have what I saw as a mature relationship with girls, without going too far.'

Throughout the world, the thriving Catholic charismatic movement is involved in a host of Vatican-approved projects and missions. In Britain, gatherings such as the annual 'New Dawn in the Church' celebrations at Walsingham, in Norfolk, attract vast crowds. Paul, now a priest, converted to Catholicism because of his early enthusiasm for the charismatic movement. 'It is tremendous for worship,' he says. 'That side of emotion needs to be taken care of – the freedom to let go, to be free, to sing in tongues, to allow all that to lift you.'

He is, however, disturbed by what he sees as a darker side to the movement. Its emphasis on 'being free and letting go' is only another way of escaping from the demands of the body, of 'mortifying' the flesh. It equates sex with evil and therefore takes pains to shut it out. 'In my group,' says Fr Paul, 'any suggestion of sexuality, and you were prayed over for deliverance. I was, because I was gay. Anything but a heterosexual outlook was anti-biblical. They were trying to deliver me from spirit-possession – the spirit of lust, the spirit of homosexuality. You get prayed over, and then you feel very free – until a little while later, you realise that there is a whole other dimension to your life that is sexual. They are failing to face up to the reality that we are whole people and that our sexuality is a vital part of who we are.'

Fr Paul, who has now broken his ties with charismatic groups, has seen in his pastoral work the damage wrought by this fundamentalist attitude. 'A young man came to me for help because he'd been involved in a cottaging offence. There were criminal proceedings and he couldn't stay with his parents. I asked a local charismatic community to take him in, on condition that they didn't ask him the nature of his problem. And, lo and behold, didn't they very subtly, out of warmth and friendship, make him feel that he "needed" to tell them? Soon they were praying over him for deliverance and he ended up worse off. His guilt about the court case was compounded by these people, who wanted to "set him free".'

At the other end of the Catholic spectrum, the polar opposite of the charismatic's noisy enthusiasm, is an organisation considered by many to be far more sinister. Opus Dei, an ultra-traditionalist movement, with a fierce anti-sexuality St Augustine himself could not have faulted, answers directly only to the Pope. Founded in Spain earlier this century by Fr Josemaria Escriva de Balaguer, this 75,000-strong fraternity enjoys a high standing in John Paul II's eyes. Its unremarkable (some have claimed decidedly shifty) founder is set to race through the Vatican's complicated saint-making process in record time. Opus Dei is keen to stress its fidelity to the teachings of the Church in all areas. It offers another channel for controlling and sublimating sexuality in the young, and replacing it with spirituality.

Opus Dei specialises in attracting young, vulnerable people, often when they arrive at university or college (you must be eighteen to join) offering them hospitality, friendship and (especially in big cities where accommodation is scarce) a secure roof over their heads. Recruiters hang around university chaplaincies, inviting people to lunches at the organisation's hostels and aiming to build upon that first link. In 1985, the Italian Parliament ordered an investigation into Opus Dei's recruitment methods, because of complaints filed by parents who claimed their children had been 'lured away'.

At first, Opus Dei offers room and board, with no strings attached. But very soon, the real cost becomes apparent. A former member describes his period with the organisation: 'Contamination from outside is avoided by censorship of magazines, newspapers, television programmes, and even members' letters to friends and family. An essential element of the spirituality of Opus Dei is the "prayer of the body" – corporal mortification. The use of the cilice and the discipline.' A cilice is a series of spiked, chain-mail links, strapped onto the thigh for two hours a day. A discipline is a small whip, used once a week in self-flagellation, while praying. Freud would have a field day.

Women and men live apart in separate hostels, the only contact being when the women enter the men's building to do domestic chores. Members go out to work, but give all their earnings to the community. In a very real sense, they abdicate all responsibility. Some go as far as taking a vow of celibacy.

The historic cult of virginity in the Catholic Church can be traced, like so much else, back to ancient Greece, where it was believed that abstaining from sex increased physical strength. Fused with Christianity, this belief turned into the notion that 'purity' meant sexual purity. Whatever your character or behaviour, the assumption is that once you enter the sexless zone, you are already halfway to heaven.

Another route for those wishing to turn their backs on sexuality is the recently revived Order of Virgins. An ancient, hermetic practice dating back to early Christianity (St Clement wrote of men and women in third-century Syria 'who have dedicated themselves to preserve their virginity for the Kingdom of Heaven'), it received renewed impetus in 1983. Number 604 in the redrafted Code of Canon Law gave official sanction to 'an order of virgins' who through 'their pledge to follow Christ more closely' consecrate their virginity to God and are 'mystically espoused to Christ'.[9] Over sixty women have, so far, taken up this option in Britain, although some bishops are known to be less than thrilled with the idea. Most recruits, who must 'never have lived in public or open violation of chastity', are in the thirty to sixty age-range, and continue to live in the world, doing everyday jobs.

What the Order of Virgins, Opus Dei and the charismatics have in common is that they all, to a greater or lesser degree, offer people – especially young people – a way of opting out of a world that the Vatican sees as lethally infected with sex. In the sanitised environments created by these organisations, sexuality is held at arm's length, as if it were a detachable, optional part of human nature. It's the nearest you can get to cutting it off and locking it away in a drawer.

Mercifully, given the side-effects, the pull of such bodies is limited, though growing. And the enthusiasm that drives people to mortify their flesh with whips and spikes does not tend to last beyond the first flush of youth – lapse figures are high in the mid-to-late twenties.

Who can blame these young people for trying to retreat from the world of sexuality altogether? For other believing Catholics, the road to romantic fulfilment is blocked by one huge obstacle. Shades of the prison house begin to close about the growing boy . . . there it stands, the Church's last line of defence against the twentieth century. The papal encyclical that effectively put the lid on Catholic female emancipation, sexual freedom within marriage and all heterosexual activity outside it. Yes, folks, it's –

Humanae Vitae

The 1968 encyclical *Humanae Vitae* made headlines around the world with its ban on artificial contraception in general, and the pill in particular. Only a few years after the Vatican II document *Gaudium et Spes* had recognised the joys of (married) sex, *Humanae Vitae* reminded Catholics that the only purpose of sexual intercourse was procreation. It stressed that the 'unitative' side of sex – the fun part – could not be separated from the 'procreative'. In other words, every time you have sex, there has to be a chance that a baby may result. That is the compulsory cocktail for Catholics – without the dash of vermouth, your glass of gin just ain't a proper dry martini.

The contraceptive pill was invented by the American Stanley Rock, a devout Catholic who believed until his dying day, in the mid-1980s, that his discovery had done mankind a Christian service. Pope Pius XI, in his encyclical *Casti Connubii*, had already declared firmly against artificial contraception, as long ago as 1930. But Rock – and millions of other Catholics – felt that the pill was different. It was not a case of sperm bashing their heads against a wall of rubber. Because it worked by altering a woman's hormonal balance, it was not, strictly speaking, a mechanical means of contraception at all. Which, many asked, was the greater sin – using mechanical methods, which prevent conception at the last fence, or taking the pill and eliminating the possibility of conception right at the start?

We have seen so many examples of traditional Catholic sexuality that it is by now easy to guess the Vatican's real objection to the pill. Here was an invention that separated sex and childbearing; that meant couples could indulge their lusts at will, even when the chemist's was shut. The pill meant, above all, that there were no more obstacles in the way of pleasurable, sinful sex without consequences.

In recent years, the pill has taken a dive in popularity, because of the reports of medical side-effects. The Church has seized upon these with a relish that is all the more unseemly because we all know the real reason behind it. As one Catholic feminist puts it: 'When I hear them moralising about the medical dangers of the pill, it makes me want to scream – the Church is out to prove that all contraception is wrong. It doesn't give a toss about women's health.'

The present generation of young Catholics does not appear to give a toss about *Humanae Vitae*. Even when they feel guilt and unease about breaking the rules, the big decision is whether or not to have sex. Since you may as well be hanged for a sheep as for a lamb, using reliable contraception is only one step down the road. At this stage in their lives, these young people do not want to be saddled with babies. Their parents tend to take the same, pragmatic approach. They may disapprove of pre-marital sex, but feel the sin of contraception is better than the conception of an unwanted child.

Some parents and teachers, however, continue to fight vigorously for *Humanae Vitae*. Joanne, now in her mid-twenties, remembers a nun swearing to her that condoms were fatally unreliable. 'She said we'd all end up pregnant. That was a great deterrent. I used to buy a pack of condoms and wash each one out before having sex with my boyfriend, to check it wasn't full of holes.' Notice that this chronic anxiety was not severe enough to put Joanne off extra-marital sex. People will do it – and they were doing it long before the present, permissive era.

St Augustine, author of so much of the Catholic Church's sexual pessimism, knew all about the problems of contraception. By his day, it had already been around for centuries – ancient Egyptian documents, from 1900 BC to 1100 BC, speak of vaginal tampons coated in acacia gum, honey or crocodile dung.[10] Before his conversion to Christianity, Augustine and his mistress used the rhythm method. It worked no better for fourth-century saints than it does for twentieth-century sinners, and it resulted for Augustine in the birth of a son.

When he saw the light in 386, Augustine – possibly guilty about his cast-off mistress, and still pervaded by the Manichaean hostility to the body – launched the Catholic conviction that sex was only for procreation within marriage.

In the twelfth century, St Thomas Aquinas picked up the baton and ran with it enthusiastically, coining the idea of Natural Law. As we outlined in Chapter One, Natural Law means that humans should imitate the sexual behaviour of animals. 'Thomas believed in mandatory compliance with nature's instructions to all living creatures,' writes Uta Ranke-Heinemann, 'and these could best be inferred from the behaviour of animals. The most important message he derived from the animal kingdom is still binding upon the Catholic Church, even today. Animals mate for reproductive reasons alone: from this we can infer the purpose of the human sexual act. Animals use no contraceptives: from this we can infer that contraceptive devices are unnatural. Such are the articles of faith to which Thomas's pseudo-theological brand of behavioural science gave rise.'[11]

Natural Law still holds sway, despite subsequent discoveries about the sex lives of animals, which rather spoil the theory. Homosexuality, for example, is common among other species besides ours. Aquinas would have had to tie himself in theological knots to explain that one.

In any case, people have always tried to sidestep Natural Law. Coitus interruptus was, for many centuries, a favourite method, though the Bible frowns upon men who spill their seed upon the ground. Condoms, made from the bladders of sheep and goats, have been around since Egyptian times. In 1843, with the vulcanisation of rubber, came the condom as we know it today. It appeared at a time when the ideas of an Anglican priest, Thomas Malthus, were gaining ground among British intellectuals. Malthus' 'Essay on the Principle of Population' (1798) demonstrated that the population was outstripping food supply. His solution was radical – that society should stop keeping the helpless alive with charity, so that only strong and useful people survived, while the weak died off naturally.

Many of his fellow-Christians were, of course, horrified by the suggestion, but there was a population explosion and the country was in the grip of a recession. People began to see the economic wisdom of birth control. The Vatican, meanwhile, declared the new-fangled rubber condom out of bounds within ten years of its appearance.

During the latter half of the nineteenth century, particularly in Europe and America, support for birth control intensified with the growth of feminism. Early champions of women's rights campaigned to release women from the very real dangers of endless childbearing. The Vatican stepped up its opposition accordingly. In 1916, at the height of the First World War, Rome was busily railing against the condom and telling women they should resist a man brandishing one as they would a rapist.

The Anglicans were the first to give an enlightened lead in the field of contraception. At the 1930 Lambeth Conference of Bishops, they decided to drop their objections to birth control. It was this decision that prompted Pius XI's vehement *Casti Connubii* (Of Chaste Spouses) mentioned above. Pius hit out at married couples who 'are weary of children and wish to gratify their desires without the consequent burden'. But oh dear, no – 'each and every marriage act must remain open to the trans- mission of life'.[12]

In 1951, however, his successor Pius XII made an important concession. Addressing Italian midwives, he admitted that it was sometimes advisable for couples to space the birth of their children. The solution was the rhythm method – known as the 'Vatican Roulette' because of its unreliability. Augustine and Aquinas would have hotly disputed the propriety of this so-called 'natural' birth control, but the Church was under pressure from rapidly developing contraceptive technology. It had to come up with something, and judged this to be the least of the available evils.

So, for forty years, Catholic couples have been grappling with this complicated system of identifying the woman's fertile period and avoiding having sex on those days. We will look at it in greater detail in our chapter on marriage – with its ther- mometers, charts and periods of abstinence, it is very unlikely to appeal to young people in the first stages of exploring their sexuality.

For them, the most attractive forms of contraception are the condom or the pill. When the latter began to be used in the late 1950s and early 1960s, an active lobby pressed for its use by Catholics to be discussed at the Second Vatican Council. These were days of hope, when the Church seemed to be on the brink of limitless reform. Pope Paul VI decided to rule on the matter himself. He did, however, in line with the liberal flavour of the times, set up a commission of theologians and lay people – including married couples – to advise him. Their report, never officially published but widely leaked, came down in favour of allowing the pill within marriage.

Their chosen remit was 'responsible parenthood'. Advocating the 'personal responsibility of each individual', and warning against 'concrete moral norms [. . .] pushed to an extreme', the majority of the commission upheld the traditional teaching that 'conjugal love and fecundity are in no way opposed, but complement each other in such a way that they constitute an almost indivisible unity.'[13] Almost indivisible – the report added that couples must decide how many children they can emotionally, physically and economically nurture.

Other important factors quoted were 'social changes in matrimony and the family, especially in the role of the woman; lowering of the infant mortality rate; new bodies of knowledge in biology, psychology, sexuality and demography; a changed estimation of the value and meaning of human sexuality and of conjugal relations'.[14]

Equally stressed was the fact that the morality of sex between couples is based on the 'ordering of their actions to a fruitful married life', which, of course, includes 'responsible, generous and prudent parenthood'. It is not based, the report added, 'upon the direct fecundity of each and every particular act'.[15] The authors were making a case for breaking the link between sex and procreation in individual bouts of lovemaking, while maintaining procreation as an overall principle.

Such typically Catholic hair-splitting should have appealed to the Vatican, as should the reverential tone of the report and its abhorrence of abortion and sterilisation. It did not. In *Humanae Vitae*, Paul VI rejected the commission's attempt to redefine modern marriage. He preferred the time-honoured wisdom of Augustine and Aquinas.

His verdict was not only a bitter disappointment to many Catholics. It was also a shock. Vatican II had given the laity a new confidence in their ability to affect decision-making at the highest level. Now, they realised that in the highly personal area of sexuality, the message was no change. With hindsight, *Humanae Vitae* can be seen as the first significant step backwards, after the radical advances of Vatican II. The spirit of reform that characterised the Second Vatican Council is absent from *Humanae Vitae*.

Paul VI is reported to have wept at the angry reaction to his letter. 'I wanted to put forward a Gospel message!' he protested to his advisers. But though *Humanae Vitae* is a most lyrical document, eloquently upholding the value of human life, few people bothered reading that far. All they wanted to know was whether the pill was allowed by the Church, and it was not.

It was not only the laity who protested. There was widespread dissent and anger among Catholic priests, many of whom left their orders. In 1968, Cardinal Patrick Boyle suspended forty-four Washington priests for questioning the wisdom of *Humanae Vitae*.[16] Papal authority had suffered a crippling blow.

David Rice, in his book *Shattered Vows* recalls the dilemma *Humanae Vitae* presented to priests in the confessional. At that time, he was a Dominican priest in Kilkenny, Ireland. A young married woman came to him for permission to use the pill:
' "He's awfully good to me when he gets it – y'know what I mean, Father. But if I refuse him, he beats me up and then he does it with the dog." ' Presumably holding onto his last meal with some difficulty, Rice took what was, for him, a momentous decision. ' "Go and use the pill," I told her. "And never mention it to a priest again." To myself I said, I'll have to face God for my disobedience, but she'll be off the hook.'[17] Rice identifies *Humanae Vitae* as a crucial turning-point in the attitude of many priests to the wisdom of the Vatican. It is debatable whether the Church has ever recovered from the battle.

Catholic newspapers that dared to question papal authority

were banned in parishes. Such was the level of interest that the English Catholic leader of the time, Cardinal Heenan, appeared on television to be grilled by David Frost. A somewhat hot and bothered Heenan appeared to suggest that there was room for debate on the subject, though he later denied this.

The dissent continues to this day. In 1989, several hundred central European theologians, including some normally noted for unswerving loyalty to Rome, publicly petitioned for a change in the teaching.[18]

For nearly twenty-five years, the Vatican's response to such appeals has been short and consistent – No. In his 1981 encyclical *Familiaris Consortio*, John Paul II underlined the message of Paul VI, though he did make concessions on the question of 'natural' contraception. St Augustine had damned Vatican Roulette, but John Paul extolled its virtues. 'The choice of the natural rhythms involves accepting the cycle of the person, that is, the woman, and thereby accepting dialogue, reciprocal respect, shared responsibility and self-control.'[19] A small change to make after 1500 years, but a change nonetheless.

It cannot be said too often, however, that the most important result of *Humanae Vitae* was the revolt among the laity. Vast numbers of ordinary Catholics took control of their sex lives back into their own hands. The teaching is rejected as unrealistic in poll after poll throughout the developed world.

A woman quoted in the Hornsby-Smith survey sums up the anger felt by many. 'It's the nuns and priests who preach, who don't get married [. . .] they think the more babies you have, the more little Catholics you'll have.'[20] Another took her tone from the dissent in clerical ranks. 'One is not really going against the Church if you use contraception [. . .] I'm going according to the bishops and the priests, who leave it up to yourself, to your conscience.'[21] A third simply felt her body was her own business. 'I don't agree with a little man sitting in Rome on a golden throne telling me that I can't take the pill if I want to [. . .] that's a business between me and God.'[22]

Disagreement with *Humanae Vitae* reaches high places. The notoriously fecund Victoria Gillick, who marched under the banner 'Roman Catholic Mother of Ten' attempted in 1984 and 1985 to stop doctors prescribing the pill to girls under sixteen without their parents' knowledge and consent. English bishops refused to back her wholeheartedly. Although not at all keen on young girls having early pre-marital sex, they had learnt from the whole *Humanae Vitae* experience that making something illegal did not stop people doing it. On numerous occasions, Mrs Gillick denounced the bishops for their lukewarm response to her campaign.

Hard on the heels of the fuss surrounding *Humanae Vitae*, the AIDS pandemic has presented the Catholic Church with another moral problem. Here, once again, it is speared on the horns of the dilemma between ideal and reality. Deep in the Catholic heart is the conviction that if the world had listened to it in the first place, AIDS would not exist. The best way to avoid getting the disease is to abstain from sexual intercourse, in the best Catholic fashion.

But it is too late for 'I told you so'. Human nature being what it is, the second best way to counteract AIDS is to sport that old *bête-noire*, a condom. Some Church leaders are backing this practical advice, while others attack the 'safe sex' messages given by health educationalists. By and large, the Vatican has refrained from reacting to AIDS in its usual hobnailed-boot fashion, but the argument has further sidelined the Christian message, and reinforced the Church's public image as anti-sex watchdog.

The proposals in 1991 to extend the distribution of condoms in Ireland drew angry responses from Church leaders. When the government suggested making condoms more widely available to anyone over sixteen (as opposed to over-eighteens, and then through a very limited network of agents) Jeremiah Newman, Bishop of Limerick, was quick to hit back at the health minister. 'Those countries of Europe where condoms are available here, there and everywhere,' he stated, 'are infested with the disease.'[23] The traditionalist line is that just as contraceptives cause abortions, rather than preventing them, they also cause AIDS. Beneath this was the subliminal message that those who screw around deserve to get AIDS anyway. This is the sort of message the liberal wing of the Church feels it can do without.

Perhaps Bishop Newman should meditate on the statistic quoted by Brenda Maddox in her pamphlet on the Church and contraception. Ireland, she says, with its Catholic stranglehold on the distribution of condoms, has the highest AIDS incidence per head of the population in the EEC.[24]

Homosexuality

AIDS has, inevitably, aggravated the dispute in the Church over one particular area of sexual morality – homosexuality. An estimated 5–10 per cent of the population are gay or lesbian.[25] For these people, coming to terms with the sexual side of life can be intensely painful.

Before 1861, British homosexual men (lesbianism has never been illegal here) faced the death penalty, if caught. At the end of the last century, the Irish poet, Oscar Wilde, was sentenced to two years of hard labour, after a sensational trial which whipped up a storm of homophobia, and forced most of London's *fin de siècle* gay scene to flee to the continent.

Since 1967, homosexual acts between consenting adult males of twenty-one and over have been legal. Despite a greater degree of acceptance, however, male and female homosexuals still have to live with a great deal of prejudice, ranging from covert discrimination to violent attacks. Thanks to AIDS, the spread of which is largely (and inaccurately) blamed on gay men, homosexuals are once more victims of mistrust, fear and open hatred.

Being a Catholic as well as a homosexual is no easy matter. As usual, the statute-books of Catholic-dominated Ireland, where homosexuality is still illegal, reflect the Vatican's attitude. The Church will only sanction sex which can transmit life, so you can imagine what it thinks about acts between persons of the same sex. In the late seventies, cracks began to appear in the crust of prejudice. These closed ten years later, as part of the worldwide reaction to AIDS. Never mind transmitting life – many in the Church held that homosexuals were transmitting death.

74

Those who believe homosexuality to be a sin can cite various Bible passages as backup. There is the stern ruling in the Old Testament: 'Thou shalt not lie with mankind as with womankind, it is abomination.' (Leviticus 22:18.) In the New Testament, there are the letters of St Paul:

Men [. . .] giving up normal relations with women, are consumed with passion for each other, men doing shameful things with men and receiving in themselves due reward for their perversion.

Romans, 1:26–27

Do you not realise that people who do evil will never inherit the kingdom of God? Make no mistake – the sexually immoral, idolaters, adulterers, the self-indulgent, sodomites [. . .] none of these will inherit the kingdom of God.

1 Corinthians 6:9

Laws are not framed for people who are upright. On the contrary, they are for criminals and the insubordinate, for the irreligious and the wicked, for the sacreligious and godless; they are for people who kill their fathers or mothers and for murderers, for the promiscuous, homosexuals, kidnappers, for liars and for perjurors – and for every else that is contrary to the sound teaching that accords with the gospel of the glory of the blessed God.

1 Timothy 1:9–10

St Paul wrote his epistles with an urgent sense that the world was disintegrating into wickedness, and that its end was nigh. Homosexuality was customary and even countenanced in ancient Graeco-Roman society – Zeus, king of all the gods on Olympus, kidnapped gorgeous Ganymede to be his cup-bearer, showing he liked a comely boy as much as a pretty girl. By the first century, the Roman empire was in decline. St Paul was not the first to identify homosexuality as a symptom of decay. As always, however, it is important to separate the thoughts of St Paul from the directives left to us by Jesus Christ.

What Christ said about Homosexuality

Nothing.

Hallowe'en

Christians seeking to overturn prejudice against homosexuality point to Christ's silence on the subject. (When he refers, in Luke 10, to the sin of Sodom, he is clearly interpreting it as a lack of hospitality.[26]) Those liberals within the Catholic Church who dispute the ruling that all sex must be procreative naturally wish to remove the sting of sin from homosexual relationships. It is a contentious area, particularly when one considers the high proportion of homosexuals in presbyteries, monasteries and convents. Dr Elizabeth Stuart, convener of the Catholic Caucus of the Lesbian and Gay Christian movement, writes: 'It has been estimated that at least 33 per cent of all priests and religious in the Roman Catholic Church in the United States are homosexual.'[27] If this statistic is anything to go by, the percentage of homosexuals bound by religious vows in the US is three times greater than the percentage of homosexuals in the country as a whole. Unsurprisingly, therefore, there is a great deal of covert sympathy for homosexuality in the Church hierarchy.

Many bishops in Britain and America recognise the foolishness of setting their faces too severely against homosexuals, since they cannot afford to alienate a third of their personnel. It is tacitly accepted that, as with any profession where the sexes are separated, the Church attracts a high number of people with homosexual inclinations. In liberal quarters, it is also accepted that this does not make them any worse at their jobs.

The 1975 Vatican Declaration on sexual ethics reiterated the strict teaching of the Church:

> At the present time there are those who, basing themselves on observations in the psychological order, have begun to judge indulgently, and even to excuse completely, homosexual relations between certain people. This they do in opposition to the constant teaching of the Magisterium and to the moral sense of the Christian people [. . .] homosexual acts are intrinsically disordered and can in no case be approved of.[28]

Alongside this directive, however, were tiny hints of leniency.

> In the pastoral field, these homosexuals must certainly be treated with understanding and sustained in the hope of overcoming their personal difficulties and their inability to fit into society. Their culpability will be judged with prudence. [. . .] In Sacred Scripture they are condemned as a serious depravity and even presented as the sad consequence of rejecting God. This judgement of Scripture does not of course permit us to conclude that all those who suffer from this anomaly are personally responsible for it.[29]

Small enough windows of tolerance, perhaps, but the liberal element in the Church dived through them eagerly. Immediately, some of the top brass in Rome saw that the 1975 Declaration had not been strict enough. Pastoral 'understanding' was being taken too far. In *An Introduction to the Pastoral Care of Homosexual Persons* (1979), the Roman Catholic bishops of England and Wales even declared that 'Homosexuality (or homophilia) as such is neither morally good or bad. It is morally neutral.'[30] Homosexuals were being soothed and encouraged by the Church. The distinction between the homosexual him/herself and homosexual 'genital acts' was blurring.

In 1986, the AIDS panic at its height, the Church clamped down. Cardinal Ratzinger's 'Letter to the Bishops of the Catholic Church on the Pastoral Care of Homosexuals' made it clear that: 'Although the particular inclination of the homosexual person is not a sin, it is a more or less strong tendency ordered towards an intrinsic moral evil.'[31] You can, in other words, be a homosexual – but you're on the wrong side of the law the moment you decide to do something about it. Because Ratzinger's ruling appeared in late October, furious homosexuals dubbed it 'The Hallowe'en Letter'.

Where Scriptural condemnation of homosexuality was in short supply, the Cardinal fell back on the classic Catholic justification of the Magisterium – that the tradition of the living body of the Church is as important as Scripture itself: 'The Scriptures are not properly understood when they are interpreted in a way which contradicts the Church's living Tradition. To be correct, the interpretation of Scripture must be in substantial accord with the Tradition.'[32] To a liberal theologian, there is an essential and maddening flaw in this age-old argument – if some barking mad medieval Pope had ordered us all to paint our bums green, the fact that Christ said nothing about green bums would be neither here nor there. Not having a green bum would be against the Magisterium of the Church, and therefore against Holy Scripture.

'Increasing numbers of people today, even with the Church,' Ratzinger complained, 'are bringing enormous pressure to bear on the Church to accept the homosexual condition as though it were not disordered and to condone homosexual activity.'[33] This can be interpreted as his swipe against Church-backed support groups for homosexuals, such as the British organisation, Quest. Ratzinger calls upon bishops to stop these groups meeting on Church premises, because 'a truly pastoral approach will appreciate the need for homosexual persons to avoid the near occasions of sin.'[34]

The duty of ministers, says the Cardinal, is to encourage homosexuals to lead a chaste life. 'The self-denial of homosexual men and women with the self-sacrifice of the Lord will constitute for them a source of self-giving which will save them from a way of life which constantly threatens to destroy them.'[35]

The tone of this letter shows how difficult it is now to be a homosexual and a devout Catholic; part of a Church which officially holds your sexual orientation to be 'evil' and 'disordered', and bars you from ever having a sexual relationship with another person. Many homosexuals within the Church argue that a person's sexuality is an inseparable part of their character. Condemn the sexuality, they say, and you condemn the whole person. They have not made a choice about the way they are, but are as God made them.

'To label a person's sexuality as disordered is to label all their relationships disordered,' writes Dr Elizabeth Stuart, 'not just those which find expression in sexual intercourse, and this includes a person's relationship with herself and with Christ.'[36]

Cardinal Ratzinger is having none of this. 'What is at all costs to be avoided is the unfounded and demeaning assumption that the sexual behaviour of homosexual persons is always and totally compulsive and therefore inculpable.'[37] Gays and lesbians, he implies, must carry their load of blame, and know that they are homosexual because they are wicked.

The indigestible kernel of Ratzinger's letter is tucked away in a single sentence, but homosexuals choked on it nonetheless: 'Even when the practice of homosexuality may seriously threaten the lives and well-being of a large number of people, its advocates remain undeterred and refuse to consider the magnitude of the risks involved.'[38] Clearly, homosexuals must also carry the responsibility for AIDS – though, as Dr Stuart points out, lesbians are far less likely to be infected with HIV than heterosexual couples.

Just when the lives of Catholic homosexuals appeared to be getting easier, the Hallowe'en Letter appeared, intent on shoving them all back into the closet and padlocking the door. 'As a result,' writes Dr Stuart, 'a number of gay and lesbian Catholic groups were evicted from Church property, constructive dialogues between gay and lesbian Catholics and members of the Church hierarchies ceased and some openly gay and lesbian

Catholics were denied the Sacraments. Large numbers of gay and lesbian people no longer felt safe in the Catholic Church [. . .] within the last year, Rome has ruled that all those offering themselves for the priestly or religious life must be screened for possible homosexual orientation, and only those homosexuals who hate their sexuality will be allowed to continue their studies.'[39]

The fact that Ratzinger felt it necessary to speak so strongly against homosexuality can be seen as a symptom of how much attitudes within the Church have softened since the general reforms of Vatican II. In the early 1960s, the gay author Michael Carson was still being taught by the Christian Brothers the rules of the Penny Catechism, that sodomy was one of the Four Sins Crying to Heaven for Vengeance (the others are wilful murder, oppression of the poor and defrauding labourers of their wages). 'If you're told you're sinful because of what you are,' says Carson, 'you end up feeling you might as well lay sin on sin. Your choice was to renounce your homosexuality or your Catholicism.'

Today's young homosexual Catholic is likely to encounter far more understanding and sympathy from the Church. As we have seen, the official line is one thing and the individual's relationship with his or her priest quite another. However, the situation is still bitter and confusing. This letter from an eighteen-year-old gay Catholic, published in the *Catholic Herald* in 1991, bears poignant witness:

> I am a devout Catholic. I am also gay. I became fully aware of my sexual orientation about three years ago when I was fifteen. I can't say that I glorified in the discovery, yet neither was I particularly distressed; it was just me – another one of the facets, the qualities, that make me the person I am.
>
> Paradoxically, perhaps, given the anti-homosexual teaching of the Church, I retained, and still retain, the implicit faith and trust in God and Catholicism that I had had up to that point. However, with the passing of puberty and the first true feelings of sexual awakening encountered by everyone, I realised what a burden had been put on me. While my friends

were talking of girlfriends and expressing interest in the
female sex, I had to keep quiet and try not to appear
conspicuous.

Loneliness must be one of the prime characteristics of
homosexuality as, while life goes on as normal, it runs
parallel with an isolated hole whenever sexual matters are
mentioned.[40]

Despite his unhappiness, this young man was prepared to accept
the teachings of the Church, and not have sex. 'I know in myself
that I will never indulge in any act of gay sex. Yet, at the same
time, I am human and, try as I might, I cannot fulfil a life of
chastity. I have had a relationship with a male friend, yet it was
understanding and loving – there was nothing dirty and sordid
about it. There doesn't have to be.'[41]

It is difficult for enlightened and sympathetic Church leaders,
faced with cases like this, to be tied to the official line. Yet tied
they are. Mario Conti, Bishop of Aberdeen, clearly trying hard to
soften the blow, recently wrote: 'Homosexuality is not a sin, but
homosexual acts are. This is what the Church teaches, and she
had no option if she is to be faithful to Revelation [. . .] Hardly a
blessed state, most certainly a pastoral situation calling for the
most sensitively kind and clearly directed pastoral care.'[42] Pastoral care is all very well, say many homosexuals, but why apply a
sticking-plaster where there is no wound?

Bishop Conti's sympathetic tone should be contrasted with
that of the Midlands prelate, who bluntly told a member of
Catholic Lesbian and Gay Caucus: 'It's no good fucking your
boyfriend on Saturday night and then going to Holy Communion
the next morning.' Or that of the Polish primate, Cardinal Glemp,
who in 1991 referred to homosexuals as 'backyard mongrels'.[43]

So the iron link between sex and procreation affects much
more than the question of contraception. Cardinal Ratzinger's
letter takes us back to St Thomas Aquinas, and the Natural Law.
'Homosexual activity is not a complementary union, able to
transmit life; and so it thwarts the call to a life of that form of self-
giving that the Gospel says is the essence of Christian living.'[44]

This ignores the central plank of the liberal's argument for toleration of homosexuality – the teaching that each person is made 'in the image and likeness of God'. This is also the argument put forward by feminists in favour of women priests, that they can be the representatives of Christ at the altar because they, too, are made in God's image. One can surely be forgiven for thinking that the hierarchy regards God's image as that of a heterosexual, celibate male in a cassock.

'You know the old Catechism question, Who made you?,' says Simon, a former seminarian now involved in putting over the Church's social justice message. 'The answer is, God made me. And I feel that God made me this way. Whatever the insecurities of the Church or anybody else about my sexual orientation, those insecurities can't be part of God.'

Simon knows he is unusual in feeling comfortable about coming out within the Catholic Church. 'I realise that many gay Catholics just turn their backs on the Church, and I can't blame them for doing so. I was lucky, because my time in the seminary gave me the ability to work out a position of dissent which, at the moment, I feel I can hold with some integrity.'

Much of the debate about the position of gay Catholics focuses upon America, homeland of the Gay Liberation movement, where homosexuality is not so much of a hidden issue as it remains in Europe. In the land of the free, it is possible to find sympathetic priests, who will conduct ceremonies of blessing for gay couples intent on lifelong partnership.

Such a notion is abhorrent to the Vatican. On most matters of sexual morality, they appear to regard Catholics as plaster saints, with never a rude thought crossing their minds. With homosexuals, they see only pederasty and promiscuity. Never mind that the majority of child-molesters are heterosexual. Never mind that countless gay Catholics, far from being promiscuous, yearn for the Church to bless their committed relationships. Never mind that many bishops, all over the world, have begged for a change of attitude. The Vatican remains adamant.

Rome offers little guidance to men and women who wish to live what Michael Carson calls 'the good gay life'. All it can say to them is – don't. At least for heterosexuals, once married and sticking to Natural Law, sexual intercourse is permitted.

Kevin has lived for many years with his partner, Robert, in south London. Both are active Catholics who would like to get more involved in parish life, but they feel shut out. 'Priests go out of their way now to talk to heterosexual couples living together,' Kevin says, 'to be more welcoming, less judgemental, especially if one of them is a Catholic. Most priests now seem to accept that people will have sexual relationships before marriage, and they are therefore more prepared to put in time to nurture them. With gay couples, there is more often just hostility. Some have to choose carefully where to take Communion. They fear being turned away at the altar rails.'

One advocate of blessings for homosexual 'marriages' is Fr Bernard Lynch, a New York priest who works with those living under the shadow of HIV/AIDS. He has challenged the conservative view taken by the Vatican and certain Church leaders in the USA – notably Cardinal John O'Connor of New York, who ordered that gay men dying of AIDS should be refused the last rites until they had repented of their 'sin'.

'Distance is a very close word for the attitude of the authorities in New York to me,' Fr Lynch says cheerfully. 'I think they would like me to be the first priest to volunteer for the space shuttle.' He feels that the 1986 letter was a step backwards in the slow and painful process of getting the Church to accept homosexuality. 'The Church used to be a little more ambivalent. That ambivalence isn't there since the Ratzinger letter. It is OK to be homosexual, but don't practice it – most homosexuals would say the same thing about Catholicism right now. It is a very sick brand of Christianity that tells gay and lesbian people they're disordered in their nature, evil in their love. Yes, the people I work with are very angry, and I'm very angry, and I'll go on being angry until the College of Cardinals elects the first lesbian pope.'

For Fr Bernard, the gap between official teaching and the lives of Catholics has become a matter of life and death when it comes to homosexuality. 'The Church is a conduit to AIDS in that the only option it gives gay people is perpetual celibacy or perpetual promiscuity. The Church is actively promoting the life-destruction of gay people. It has blood on its hands. When I celebrate Mass, I ask my community not to call to mind their sins, but the sins committed against them; and to forgive the Church for the way it has oppressed us in this, our hour of greatest need.'

The Vatican distinction between natural and unnatural, 'orientation' and 'genital expression' angers Fr Bernard. 'It is natural for a gay person to be attracted to his own gender, and it is natural for a person who hasn't got the gift of celibacy to express their sexuality with their own gender. It's unnatural for them if they do it with the opposite gender.'

Fr Bernard is a rarity; a gay priest who has risked his career to speak out. There are many more who prefer to stay in the closet, for fear of losing their parishes and becoming the first missionaries on the moon. Taking religious vows, and the commitment to lifelong celibacy these entail, is the other option for young Catholics in the official rulebook. You may get married and produce children, or you may consecrate your life to the service of God.

Four:
Tending
to Perfection

Among all human affection, the human spirit is especially held fast by married love . . . consequently the marriage bond is to be avoided at all costs by those tending to perfection.

St Thomas Aquinas 'On the Perfection of Spiritual Life'

Deprive the Church of honourable marriage and you will fill her with concubinage, incest and all manner of nameless vices and uncleanness.

St Bernard of Clairvaux[1]

A priest should know everything there is to know about sexuality, short of experience.

John Thomas, US Jesuit

During the 1990 Rome gathering of world bishops to discuss the state of the priesthood, a Brazilian cardinal revealed to the assembled throng of ecclesiastical bigwigs that he had got the green light from Pope John Paul II to ordain two married men.

The motivation behind this rare concession on the part of the Vatican was plain. In Brazil, the largest Catholic nation in the world, there is a desperate shortage of priests to say Mass and administer the Sacraments – approximately one per every 10,000 faithful, compared with one per 950 in Italy, according to the latest Vatican Statistical Yearbook.[2] In the Amazon diocese of São Felix do Araguia, the size of Britain and Ireland, just fourteen

87

priests, most of them ageing European missionaries, struggle to get round each scattered Catholic community at least once a year.

The Brazilian cardinal, Alosio Lorscheider, pointed out that to resort to married men of proven virtue – *viri probati* – not only made good practical sense, but revived an earlier practice of the Church. He had the all-important legal precedent to back him, and his need for priests was urgent.

The very next day, however, the Vatican stepped in with a hasty clarification. Yes, it had given permission to ordain the two married men, but the Holy Father had insisted that they must live with their spouses as brother and sister.

The official message was clear – both to the assembled bishops searching for ways to tackle the crippling shortage of vocations to the priesthood and to Catholics worldwide. Rome was reminding them that whatever wild remedies were forced upon them by the priest-famine, marriage and ordination remain two entirely separate sacraments. Priest is priest and sex is sex, and never the twain shall meet.

To lay Catholics, the Holy See was saying, in effect: We know that in theory, being a priest and being a husband are vocations of equal worth. But when it comes to the crunch, we know which one we prefer.

The bishops were not slow to read the signs of the times. Various delegates made impassioned pleas for a married priesthood. Another Brazilian bishop, Valfredo Tepe of Ilheus, warned the synod that in his country 'there are not enough authentically celibate vocations for the many communities in danger of falling prey to [evangelical] sects.'[3] But the final communiqué of the gathering showed the Church still buried in the ostrich position.

The principal consideration was the 'sign value' of a celibate ministry. This was more important than the fact that by the year 2000 over half Brazil's Catholics would be starved of the sacraments from one year to the next. Receiving the sacraments from the hand of a married man is, apparently, worse than no sacraments at all.

The synod's declaration is not the final word. Pope John Paul will produce a document from their deliberations. The chances of a road-to-Damascus conversion, however, are slender. The present Pope is not in the habit of changing his mind and, where anything remotely sexual is concerned, he is adamantine.

During his pontificate, men and women with a vocation to the religious or priestly life will continue to make two decisions. The first is to seek ordination to the priesthood or decide to enter a religious order. The second is to renounce all thoughts of sex. Catholic priests and nuns are not allowed to do it. Their sexless state is supposed to shine as a beacon of example to the laity. An earthly bond with another human being is held to distract them from the work of God. Upon his ordination, a priest pledges an oath (a vow if he joins an order) of celibacy. Here, we should make a distinction between celibacy and chastity. Celibacy means the single state, chastity means no sex. In effect, however, if you are living by the rules of the Catholic Church, the meaning is the same.

This is the ideal. There are signs that the reality is, as usual, somewhat different. A 1990 survey by Richard Sipe, a psychiatrist at John Hopkins University, Baltimore, revealed that 20 per cent of US priests were having sex at any one time. Only 2 per cent were truly chaste.[4]

A vocation and what the Church reverently terms the 'gift' of celibacy do not necessarily go together. As Alan, a former seminarian, demands: 'Why, when the Church is so logical in so many things – indeed, is hidebound by logic – does it live by the logic that celibacy is a unique gift *and* that everyone not married is expected to have it?'

Fr Richard McKay, a Bristol priest in his early forties, emphasises the practical cost of this double step. 'At the tender age of eighteen, I resigned my right to have a sex life. It wasn't a free choice, and if things were different I would probably have a wife and children by now. Celibacy is my lot. Not because I chose it, but because I chose to follow the call of God. From my early teens, I knew I should be a Catholic priest. Unfortunately for me, and for many other men who follow what they believe to be their true vocation, the Church still insists on compulsory celibacy. So it comes as a package. If you choose the priesthood, you inevitably have to embrace the celibate life too.'

Fr Richard's candour is unusual, but his views are not uncommon among the priests we have spoken to. We should add, in fairness, that many also spoke in favour of the rule of celibacy – there are positive as well as negative aspects. Before we go into these, however, we should consider how it came about in the first place, this rule that Fr Richard describes as 'a centuries-old experiment run by the Catholic Church, which should now be deemed to have failed'.[5]

Eunuchs for Heaven

So much hangs upon Christ's discussion with his disciples in Matthew 19, concerning marriage, divorce and celibacy, that it is worth quoting in full.

> Some Pharisees approached him, and to put him to the test they said, 'Is it against the Law for a man to divorce his wife on any pretext whatever?' He answered, 'Have you not read that the Creator from the beginning made them male and female, and that he said: This is why a man leaves his father and mother and becomes attached to his wife, and the two become one flesh? They are no longer two, therefore, but one flesh. So then, what God has united, human beings must not divide.'
>
> They said to him, 'Then why did Moses command that a writ of dismissal should be given in cases of divorce?' He said to them, 'It was because you were so hard-hearted, that Moses allowed you to divorce your wives, but it was not like this from the beginning. Now I say this to you: anyone who divorces his wife – I am not speaking of an illicit marriage – and marries another, is guilty of adultery.'
>
> The disciples said to him, 'If that is how things are between husband and wife, it is advisable not to marry.' But he replied, 'It is not everybody who can accept what I have said, but only those to whom it is granted. There are eunuchs born so from

the mother's womb, there are eunuchs made so by human
agency, and there are eunuchs who have made themselves so
for the sake of the kingdom of Heaven. Let anyone accept this
who can.'

Note the last sentence. The New Jerusalem Bible, widely used by
Catholics, draws upon St Jerome's Latin translation, the Vulgate.
In the King James Authorised Version, the seventeenth century
Church of England translation, the same sentence reads: 'He that
is able to receive it, let him receive it,' ending Christ's thoughts on
celibacy in a less commanding tone.

But does this passage mean that Christ is recommending
celibacy for the priests of the Christian Church? His words are
often quoted in this context by popes, not least John Paul II in his
1979 Maundy Thursday Letter to the Priests of the World.

The interpretation is, however, open to question. Liberal
theologians argue that Christ is talking about the renunciation of
adultery. As we have said above, his view of marriage as indissoluble was radical for his time. His disciples appear to be saying that
if you have to be tied to one woman for ever, marriage is too
awful to contemplate. If this is the true meaning, Christ's reply
seems almost shockingly easy-going: 'It is not everybody who
can accept what I have said.' Throughout the Gospels, Christ
shows a deep understanding of the repeated human failure to
live up to ideals. That chronic, inbuilt failure is the reason God
became incarnate in Christ in the first place.

The principal reason advanced for a celibate priesthood is that a
priest is Christ's representative, and Christ is assumed to have
been celibate. The only women mentioned in the Gospels,
besides his mother, are those associated with his public ministry.
However, Christ was (as many Christians have preferred to
forget) an exemplary Jew. Jewish priests are permitted – indeed,
expected – to marry, though the Old Testament rules confine
them to 'maidens' or the widows of other priests. The Jewish
theologian, Ben-Chorin, has put forward the notion that if Jesus
had been a good Jew, subject to the customs of his people, he
would himself have been married. He cites the Talmud: 'A

twenty-year-old youth who lives without a wife is visited by sinful thoughts [. . .] a man is ever in the power of the urge from which marriage alone delivers him.' Ben-Chorin goes on to quote one Rabbi Eleasar Ben-Asai: 'He that abstains from marriage transgresses the law of procreation and is to be regarded as a murderer who diminishes the number of beings created in the image of God.'[6]

The four Gospels faithfully record Christ's departures from Jewish Law. If he had flouted custom by being unmarried in his early thirties, why isn't that recorded too? 'Had he disdained marriage,' maintains Ben-Chorin, 'his Pharisaic opponents would have rebuked him for this sin of omission and his disciples would have questioned him about it.'[7]

Ben-Chorin's scholarly thesis flies in the face of nearly two thousand years of Christian tradition, and would be regarded by many as rank blasphemy. Yet the authors cannot help wondering what would be so terrible about discovering that Christ had a wife. Would the fact that the Son of God (or the Son of Man, as he preferred to describe himself) had a sexual relationship, even one blessed by God and the Law, invalidate his message?

Since before the Middle Ages, there have been legends about Christ sleeping with Mary Magdalene, whom popular history has cast as the penitent whore. This old chestnut surfaced again in Martin Scorsese's controversial 1988 feature film, *The Last Temptation of Christ*, and in the sensational blockbuster *The Holy Blood and The Holy Grail*[8] which recycled the ancient taradiddle that Christ and Mary founded the Merovingian dynasty of France. The authors consider the latter work nonsensical and vulgar. But it is interesting in that it mirrors society's attitudes to women. Those who believe Christ had sex with anyone think it must have been with Mary, because she would have been 'available'. Though there is not a shred of concrete historical evidence to support either theory, we believe that the argument advanced by Ben-Chorin is worthy of consideration.

Whether Christ was married or not, his disciples, St Paul tells us, were married men, who took their wives with them on missionary tours. Yet St Paul's Epistles, written before the

Gospels, are also held up by the Catholic Church as justification for a celibate priesthood. With the end of the world, as he thought, pressing down upon him, Paul was intensely eager for early Christians to be free from any ties which might distract them from their salvation. For this reason, he was lukewarm about marriage.

> Yes, it is a good thing for a man not to touch a woman; yet to avoid immorality every man should have his own wife and every woman her own husband [. . .] otherwise Satan may take advantage of any lack of self-control to put you to the test.
>
> 1 Corinthians 7:1–2, 5

Even stern St Paul, however, adds qualifiers to his directives.

> I am telling you this as a concession, not an order. I should still like everyone to be as I am myself; but everyone has his own gift from God, one this kind and the next something different.
>   To the unmarried and to widows I say: it is good for them to stay as they are, like me. But if they cannot exercise self-control, let them marry, since it is better to be married than to be burnt up.
>
> 1 Corinthians 7:6–9

The last phrase means, incidentally, burnt up with sexual desire, not burnt on the coals of Tophet. St Paul is saying grudgingly that he supposes people must have sex, and it is better to do it within Christian marriage. Writing about virginity, his instructions to the Corinthians are equally careful.

> About people remaining virgin, I have no directions from the Lord, but I give my own opinion as a person who has been granted the Lord's mercy to be faithful. Well then, because of

93

the stress which is weighing upon us, the right thing seems to be this: it is good for people to stay as they are. If you are joined to a wife, do not seek to be released; if you are freed of a wife, do not look for a wife. However, if you do get married, that is not a sin, and it is not sinful for a virgin to enter upon marriage.

1 Corinthians 7:25–28

St Paul goes on to remind his flock that the end of the world is nigh, and that fleshly pleasures are the last things they should have on their minds. He might well have been surprised to visit his church two thousand years on — first, to find that the world had not been swallowed in flames, second, to find so many miserable, 'burning' people pressganged into virginity in the Lord's name.

The cult of virginity, fuelled by Greek and Roman philosophy and the influence of Gnosticism, grew powerfully during the first four centuries of Christianity. 'I consider there is nothing more calculated to cast a man's spirits down from the citadel,' wrote St Augustine, 'than the blandishments of a woman.'[9] As emphasis upon the sacramental role of the priest grew, those who were having sex came to be considered impure and unworthy to handle the eucharist. In AD 385, Pope Siricius wrote to Bishop Himerius of Tarragona that it was a 'crime' for married priests to have sex after ordination. Just like his present-day successor, John Paul II, he thought priests and their wives should live together as brother and sister.

Celibacy became mandatory for priests at the Second Lateran Council in 1139. Pope Innocent II decreed that ordination was an impediment to marriage. Up to then, married priests had been the norm. Afterwards, canon law stated (and continues to state) that matrimony and celibacy were mutually exclusive. 'Virginity,' wrote St Thomas Aquinas, in his *Summa Theologiae*, 'seeks the soul's good in a life of contemplation mindful of the things of God. Marriage seeks the body's good — the bodily multiplication of the human race — in an active life in which husband and wife are mindful of the things of this world. Without doubt then the state of virginity is preferable to that of even continent marriage.'[10]

Aquinas, writing in the 1260s, was a Dominican friar, and his distinction between the contemplative and the bodily life is significant. At the time of the Second Lateran Council, religious orders, made up of men and women who had separated themselves from the world and answered directly to Rome, were gaining power and influence. The 1139 celibacy ruling can be seen as an attempt to impose on all priests the regime that was proving so successful in the burgeoning monasteries. There were also practical reasons behind the ruling. Married priests were bequeathing Church benefices to their children and enforced celibacy made the practice illegal.

Celibacy was far from popular, and there were repeated purges of clergy wives and 'concubines' throughout the next few centuries. But where a bishop was sympathetic, married Catholic priests could be found until the middle of the sixteenth century. The law was set in concrete at the Council of Trent in 1545, when the last loophole (concerning clerics who had married before ordination) was removed.

Despite the rigidity of the law, there have been surges of resistance. During the French Revolution, priests were given the right to marry. It was taken away again in 1801, when Napoleon re-established formal links with Rome. In times of upheaval, revolution or persecution, the celibacy rule is easily brushed aside.

At the moment, the Vatican is wondering what on earth to do with an estimated 300 married clergy, ordained in secret before the 1989 revolution in Czechoslovakia. The Archbishop of Prague, speaking to a Viennese newspaper in 1991, blamed 'over-excited people who were unable to evaluate the reality of the situation they faced. They thought that the communists would destroy the priesthood and so they set up parallel structures to allow the church to continue whatever happened. But they overestimated the real dangers, and that led to some married men being made priests, and one or two women.'[11]

The women, needless to say, are utterly beyond the pale. But canon lawyers have suggested that the male priests should be transferred to the Greek Catholic Church, which is an Eastern Rite Church with allegiance to Rome which still permits a married priesthood. (The Greek Church has reportedly received this suggestion with *froideur*; a case of *Timeo romanes et dona ferentes*.)

The Catholic Church is the only Christian church which insists upon a celibate priesthood. Priests of the Greek and Russian Orthodox Churches (which broke away from the See of Rome at the Council of Chalcedon in AD 451) are permitted to marry, though their higher ranks are filled by celibate monks. And, of course, Protestant priests have had wives since the great Reformation which shook Europe in the sixteenth century. Its founding father, Martin Luther (1483–1546), a former Augustinian monk, carried over a great deal of Catholic sexual morality into Protestantism, but preached the virtues of marriage for the clergy.

So is the Catholic Church wrong to insist upon a celibate priesthood, when other Christian priests have had wives for many hundreds of years? Can a married man be Christ's representative? No, say traditionalists, because Christ was unmarried, and lived a life of chastity. They base this premise partly on the Biblical quotes above, and partly on the Magisterium of the Church's history. And they will also take the line that a priest fulfils his duties better when unencumbered with a wife and children. This, too, can be traced back to St Paul's Letter to the Corinthians. 'An unmarried man can devote himself to the Lord's affairs; all he has to worry about is pleasing the Lord.'[12]

We must point out that for every priest who finds celibacy an intolerable burden, there are others who happily consecrate the sexual side of their lives to the service of God. But, as the many personal stories in David Rice's book *Shattered Vows* testify, when a priest has not freely chosen celibacy, it is more likely to be a hindrance than a help. 'There are thousands of priests,' he writes, 'completely happy with their ministry and with the Church, who quite simply fall in love and marry [. . .] the love often leads a man to a deeper ministry, rather than a desire to abandon it.'[13]

Rice proposes that secular priests (that is, priests who are not members of a religious order) should be free to marry, while 'religious orders, with their community traditions, would be the natural and supportive environment for those who choose celibacy.'[14]

The Vatican continues to oppose any change in the rules. But, as we have seen, the very rigidity of its rules tends to be reinforced by exceptions and loopholes. The eye of God may be all-seeing, but the eye of his Church has selective blindness. There are married priests today, in full communion with Rome. 'Missionaries in Peru,' writes David Rice, 'tell me that they estimate that 80 per cent of local priests live with women. [. . .] In Brazil [. . .] they estimate that between 60 per cent and 70 per cent of native Brazilian priests have some sort of liaisons with women.'[15]

In the mid-sixties, when Pope Paul VI refused to discuss the possibility of a married priesthood, he nevertheless recognised the credentials of Bishop Salamao Ferras of the Free Catholic Church of Brazil, who attended the Council with his wife. He also recognised the orders of priests of the Eastern Rite Churches.

And, in England today, a handful of married convert Anglican clergymen have been given dispensations by Rome to be ordained as Catholic priests. One such is Fr Peter Cornwell, a former Anglican now working as a prison chaplain. Unlike the Brazilian priests, Cornwell and his wife, Hilary, were not expected to live together as 'brother and sister', once Cornwell was ordained as a Catholic priest. 'My job is to show that being a married priest works without bringing the skies down,' he says. Having experienced the married state for twenty-five years, however, his approach is realistic.

'Let's not treat a married priesthood as some great new Jerusalem. The Church has a very romantic notion of celibacy, and a very romantic view of marriage. Neither will do. Reality is a much more sturdy base to build on, which is why I'm very hesitant about saying marriage is the answer to the problem. I do know celibate priests who are so by vocation, and are totally reconciled. I'm hesitant, therefore, about setting up married priests as some kind of magic. That's not the case. What we do need are priests – both married and celibate – reconciled with their sexuality.'

Fr Cornwell feels that the problem is not celibacy versus marriage, so much as the Church's collective attitude to human relationships. 'I have to recognise that there are things a celibate priest can do, which I can't,' he admits. 'I must not, for example, treat my wife and family as a sideshow, with my commitment as a priest as something that squeezes them out. I do think, however, that the two roles are reconcilable. It all depends on your theological basis – if you think that being connected with God means being unconnected with other human beings. This sets up a rivalry between love for God and love for human beings, and that is not what the Gospel is about. It is a recipe for Godliness that is a substitute for being human that creates cold, inhuman, fearful priests.' The official line is that priests like Fr Cornwell are individual exceptions, which only serve to prove the rule. Frustrated Catholic priests take the more cynical line that if you want to have your cake and eat it, you should marry, become an Anglican vicar, then convert and ask to become a Catholic priest. A complicated route, but preferable, some think, to enforced, lifelong celibacy.

Brides of Christ

When a nun takes her final vows, she walks up the aisle towards the altar, clad in a white dress and a long white veil. All nice Catholic women are supposed to marry but nuns take the ultimate husband, Jesus Christ. Joined body and soul to the Holy Spirit, many nuns wear a wedding ring, as an outward symbol of that mystical union. St Catherine of Siena (1347–1380), a Dominican nun, had a vision in which the Blessed Virgin Mary held her hand, while Christ put a ring upon it, thus espousing her to himself. The ring, though invisible to others, remained visible to Catherine. St Teresa of Avila (1515–1582) enjoyed what amounted to a society wedding, with the local nobility looking on, when she entered the Carmelite Order in 1537.

Women, as we have seen, are traditionally thought to have the greater potential for sexual sin and uncleanness. Paradoxically, as the other side of the same coin, they also have the potential for greater purity – if they 'mortify' their flesh and bind their femininity in chains. A nun's wedding vows are those of 'poverty, chastity and obedience'. Her traditional garb is a shapeless black robe, a long black veil, and a white coif or wimple to hide her neck and forehead. Her roles are various – either enclosed contemplation, teaching small children and girls or making the Pope's dinner – but she remains far below a priest in the Catholic hierarchy. She is not only a servant of Christ, but also a servant of his male servants. St Teresa of Avila wrote despondantly that 'the mere thought that I am a woman makes my wings droop'.[16]

Inside the convent walls, however, it is another story. The calendar of saints is full of women like Catherine of Siena and Teresa of Avila, who were brilliant, talented and forceful. They may have rejected the world when they took their vows, but the world would never have heard of them if they had submitted themselves to flesh-and-blood husbands.

In the Middle Ages, when the power and wealth of the monasteries were growing, taking the veil was a woman's only alternative to the slavery of marriage and child-bearing. And for a clever and ambitious woman, it could mean a satisfying career. The prioress of a convent, a well-born woman who had brought a handsome dowry to the order, would often find herself with the sole responsibility for running a thriving estate. Despite her avowed lowliness and servitude, she could – like St Catherine, St Teresa and St Hildegard of Bingen (1098–1179) – write and publish under her own name, and have a voice in Church politics. Catherine was active in resolving the 'Great Schism' between the rival popes in Rome and Avignon in 1378, and Teresa founded the Discalced or reformed Order of Carmelites.

Virginity was prized in the nuns of those days, but not absolutely necessary. Widows unable to face the prospect of another husband could take refuge in a convent. They also made useful prisons for intractable unmarried girls who had offended their families, but anyone with enough money could sidestep the harsh discipline, and lead lives of comfort and ease. Although St Teresa of Avila went to the penitential lengths of wearing a saddle and entering the convent refectory on all fours carrying another nun on her back, she was allowed to decorate her cell and receive gifts from home.

Teresa was notoriously chaste, but sex in a convent was not necessarily out of the question. The lascivious nun, hauling a man through the window of her cell at night, was a favourite figure in medieval bawdry. And tales of lesbian orgies in the convent cloisters still abound – not to mention the one about the nun and the candle, which has probably been doing the rounds since Chaucer's day.

It has often been said, too, that the emotional fervour of female saintliness has an element of sublimated sexuality. Certainly, the visions experienced by St Teresa were physical as well as spiritual. Her biographer, Shirley du Boulay, argues that Bernini's famous sculpture of the saint in ecstasy, with 'its total preoccupation with the erotic dimension of the experience at the expense of the mystical says more about Bernini than it does about Teresa.'[17] But here is the passage upon which it is based:

> It pleased the Lord that I should see this angel in the following way. He was not tall, but short, and very beautiful, his face so aflame that he appeared to be one of the highest types of angel who seem to be all afire [. . .] In his hands I saw a long golden spear and at the end of the iron tip I seemed to see a point of fire. With this he seemed to pierce my heart several times so that it penetrated to my entrails. When he drew it out, I thought he was drawing them out with it and he left me completely afire with a great love for God. The pain was so sharp that it made me utter several moans; and so excessive was the sweetness caused me by the intense pain that one can never wish to lose it, nor will one's soul be content with anything less than God. It is not bodily pain, but spiritual, though the body has a share in it – indeed a great share.[18]

Teresa, with her combination of fiery devotion and overwhelming sense of her own lowliness and sinfulness, remained a template and role-model for the Catholic nun until the mid-1960s. Then, along with so much else, the lives of monks and nuns underwent radical change after Vatican II. Many orders put aside the flapping medieval robes which have terrified so many generations of children. Today's nun is unlikely to bear much resemblance to the wimpled sisters in *The Sound of Music*. She wears a pinafore dress of grey or navy, and a simplified coif, more like a headscarf. Some go even further. One woman who re-visited her old convent school in London told us she was 'astounded' to see nuns in jeans and trainers.

The Spartan conditions of convent life also began to relax after Vatican II. It must be said that the discipline is precisely what attracts many to the religious life, and that it is still possible to find nuns who live traditional lives of privation, silence and self-mortification. But many more have elected to come out from behind the iron grille that used to separate a nun from the rest of the world.

Inevitably, the implicit feminism of the whole convent ethos has begun to come out into the open. Sister Myra Poole is a nun at the radical end of the spectrum. She feels that many of the problems of the Catholic Church are rooted in its chronic misogyny. 'Women were regarded as inferior and the cause of sin by the Fathers of the Church,' she says, 'so consequently, sex is seen as sinful and dirty by Catholics. The first thing that should be hammered home in Catholic sex education is that women are not inferior.'

Sister Myra has little time for enforced celibacy. 'The idea of a celibate male secular priesthood is completely ridiculous, and is simply a result of the Church's peculiar obsession with sex. As far as possible, a priest should be part of the congregation he works with. How can a male celibate possibly relate to the problems of a married woman?'

Like David Rice, however, she makes a distinction between secular priests, and those in religious orders. 'For monks and nuns, celibacy isn't a problem. It's part of the package of having a

101

vocation. My celibacy frees me from other responsibilities and diversions. When you realise that you have a vocation, you know that there could be no place for marriage and motherhood in your life. It ceases to be a question.'

Sister Teresa, who teaches in seminaries, shares both Sister Myra's commitment to celibacy and her conviction that Catholic attitudes to women can strew a nun's path with difficulties. 'My impression has been that the students have good and easy relationships with the women who do domestic and secretarial jobs at the seminary,' she says, 'but find it impossible to deal with women in positions of authority. Their attitude to me was initially very truculent. That might have been because it was an extra course on an already busy schedule, but there was a great deal of jocularity that was decidedly anti-feminist in tone, and especially anti-women religious. One student told me that the Church was a male institution. Go and count the number of people in the pews, I suggested. But he came back with "Ah, but it's the people in the sanctuary who matter."'

Today's seminarians are tomorrow's priests. The hostility Sister Teresa encountered from them shows that Catholic attitudes to women are still in the age of steam. She feels that as soon as one of these fledgling priests meets an intelligent, articulate woman who is neither a domestic nor a nun, 'it will be such a great event and revelation that they're in danger of running off with her.'

Nuns of the younger generation are now demanding to be taken more seriously, and to be given a more fulfilling role in the running of the Church. The writer Wendy Perriam, however, who says she can't look at a nun without wanting to shoot her, thinks the changes wrought by Vatican II are only superficial. 'I have a friend who works with nuns in a Catholic school. She says she is horrified by the bitterness and lack of love among them.'

From the ages of four to twenty-one, Perriam was surrounded by nuns and imbibed their attitudes to sex and the body. 'They had no bodies – they were just robes with hands. What I saw was limited, strained, controlled. When I was twelve, I grew breasts. Mother Benedict beckoned me into a corner, and told me I must do everything I could to hide them.' For Perriam, being a nun came to mean being bitter, repressed and wilfully out of touch with human feelings.

Having a sexual relationship and bearing children are not compatible with life in a convent. A woman who does these things may still be religious and God-fearing, but she will not be a nun. 'Ideally,' a Catholic woman theologian told us, 'there would be a married secular priesthood, outside the religious orders, which would include women priests. Celibacy is not for everyone. I believe that a married woman, a mother, has just as much to offer the Church.'

Counting the Cost

The emotional hardships caused by mandatory celibacy are costing the Church dear. The Vatican, as we have seen, does operate a limited back-door service in very special cases. But though the pleas to permit at least secular priests to marry have swelled to an insistent clamour, the sign on the front door is still 'No Change'. This intransigence seems all the stranger when we consider the crisis in the priesthood – the falling vocations, and the estimated 100,000 priests who have broken their vows over the past twenty years. Is the Church cutting its own throat?

As we reported in Chapter One, the Vicar for Religion in one English Catholic diocese claims that the vast majority of priests seeking laicisation are currently languishing in his in-tray because they fell in love and wish to marry. 'Laicisation' is the process by which Rome officially releases a priest from his vows. Until he has been through this process, he is unable to marry in a Catholic Church. (If he has thrown away his faith along with his Roman collar, he is free to marry in a registry office; a union not recognised by the Church.)

Laicisation is a complicated affair, which has to pass through layers of Vatican bureaucracy, and can take several years to complete. So we should not be surprised that bishops, when confronted with a priest who has fallen in love, often advise him to get the sex out of his system, and remain in orders – no need to burn the house down just to get a bit of toast. This is cold comfort for a priest brought up to believe in the sanctity of marriage, never mind the feelings of the woman he loves. 'The application process for laicisation is both demeaning and offensive,' writes the former priest David Rice in *Shattered Vows*. 'For the application to have the slightest chance, you have to admit to being either mad or bad, or that you should never have been a priest in the first place. In other words, that you are devoid of sexual control; or that you are a psychiatric case.'

Leaving his holy orders causes a priest a great deal of grief and pain. It is not something he will do lightly. If he has kept his faith, he feels it is vital to go through laicisation, to make his peace with God. Seen from a priest's point of view, Pope John Paul II's initial decision to stem the priestly exodus by freezing laicisations seems needlessly cruel. And it did not work – the door was barred, but priests climbed out of the window. Acknowledging failure, the laicisation ban was recently lifted. But at the highest level, no serious attempt has yet been made to find out exactly why priests are leaving in such numbers. We suspect they already know the answer.

Of the priests who have stayed, particularly those in Europe and North and South America, large numbers wish to see the rules changed. In a 1987 *New York Times*/COBS poll, 55 per cent of US priests were in favour of optional celibacy. In 1990, the *Catholic Herald* conducted a survey of delegates at the annual National Conference of Priests. 75 per cent wanted a review of mandatory celibacy – a figure that grew to 90 per cent in the younger age group.[19]

More depressing still is the shortage of vocations to the priesthood – even in Latin America, with its vibrant and dynamic Church inspired by liberation theology. In the absence of priests, young men are leading communities in Gospel-based political action, but clearly failing to see how renouncing their right to marry will serve their neighbours.

One reason for the shortage may be the diminishing of the

priest's social status, as society becomes increasingly secular. But this also applies to Protestant pastors, and they seem to be having less trouble in the recruitment department. In US Protestant seminaries, enrolment rose from 42,627 in 1979 to 58,851 in 1983 – an increase of 14.6 per cent. What do Protestant priests have that Catholics lack? Wives and families. It is hard not to see celibacy as the main reason for the unattractiveness of the Catholic ministry in the eyes of promising young men.

Joys of No Sex

There is a positive side to celibacy. Even Fr Richard McKay, the West Country priest who admitted he had to be dragged into celibacy kicking and screaming, can see it. 'I'm not arguing for a moment that celibacy doesn't have a great deal of value. If anything, the Church is undermining and negating its worth by forcing people into it. Positive celibacy can be liberating and life-giving, when we choose to live without those relationships that exclude others. It's all about loving by being alongside people. What I object to is the fact that I had no choice. In taking away that choice, the Church is, in my opinion, denying me a basic right.'

Richard entered the seminary and waved goodbye to the possibility of a sex life when he was still in his teens. Nowadays, English bishops require young men to get a job and do some ordinary living before they make a final commitment. The fact that a candidate for a seminary has a sexual history is no longer seen as a drawback. On the contrary. The more progressive rectors are adamant that they are not looking for eighteen-year-old virgins.

Andrew Maggs is one of the characters of Wonersh seminary, in the countryside outside Guildford, which serves the southern dioceses of England and Wales. A trained psychiatric nurse from the Rhondda, he first thought about being a priest when he was eighteen.

'I'd been to the careers officer and I'd chosen three things – a prison officer, a nurse and a priest. Well, I'm five foot six, so that ruled out prison officer. Nursing wasn't a thing to be done by a Welsh boy. So I went to see a priest about being a priest, and he said no, you've got to become a Catholic first, and get your A Levels.'

Crestfallen, Andrew decided to swallow his Welsh macho pride and take up nursing. Inspired by the hospital chaplaincy service, he became a Catholic. But he put all thoughts of the priesthood to one side, until he was mugged by five men who left him for dead. Six operations followed, and plastic surgery. While Andrew recovered, he thought about his future.

'I saw there was so much to do, and I wanted to give my life. I can see that is a pretty selfish way of looking at things. I couldn't give my life to the trade union movement, I couldn't give it to the Labour Party. But I could say to the Church: here I am. Do something with me.'

Andrew had lived with a girlfriend when he was working, and they were engaged for two and a half years, before a largely amicable split. But he does not see celibacy as a problem – having seen 'the other side', as he puts it, his view is resolutely pragmatic.

'This summer, I lived in a presbytery for two weeks, looking after the place because the priest's father had died. Having lived a nice, settled life with my fiancée, those two weeks in the parish were a revelation. There were sick calls, requests, Auntie Bloggs's cat up a tree, the lot. That experience and my previous relationship led me to think it's not possible to have a married priesthood. Or rather, it's possible, but one or other gets devalued.'

He argues his case from experience. 'When I was nursing, my fiancée and I went out one night. We'd had a superb time, we were in bed together. My bleep went off from the hospital. I had to decide whether to answer it, or whether to stay in bed. When I got to work the next morning, all it meant was there were forms for me to fill in. Someone else had covered. But as a priest, if I'm stuck in a parish in the Rhondda where the next parish is six miles away, and I don't fancy getting out of bed, there's nobody there to cover. When you're administering something as essential as the sacraments, you've got to be there.'

It is not, Andrew insists, merely a question of being available, like a doctor on call. 'What happens if someone comes knocking on your door at midnight, desperate for the Sacrament of Reconciliation? Do you say, "Oh, quick then, dive into the confessional and get it over with?" What if they reveal something that's going to take some real hard work and talking through? Do you say, "Hang on, the wife's going to kill me"?' The priestly role undoubtedly puts strain on a marriage, as many an Anglican vicar's wife can testify.

Andrew admits that renouncing sex is not done lightly or easily, but sees it in terms of exchanging one gift for another. As far as he is concerned, being free to serve others is potentially more rewarding than an active sex life.

'I think some people attach their own view to the single life, thinking: "What would I do if I couldn't get it?" – the Big It. And then they put that on you. You're not getting it, so you must be frustrated. They don't see the beauty that you see in celibacy.'

This is what Sister Mary Huddleston, writing in the Catholic journal *America* in 1990, identifies as the Poor Father Syndrome – the assumption that 'unless a person experiences the physical intimacy of spousal and filial relationships, that person will not be fulfilled humanly, and therefore cannot be happy in the clerical state.'[21] Frankly, Sister Mary doubts that sex is everything it's cracked up to be. 'Right off common sense can infer that if genital intimacy were as satisfying as it is reputed to be, the world would be an unbounded ocean of bliss.'[22]

No, the world is not an ocean of bliss. But we must point out that Sr Mary is writing from the traditional Catholic assumption that sex is a kind of luxury, like chocolates, easy to renounce if we are sufficiently high-minded. She makes little allowance for the fact that satisfying or not, genital intimacy makes the world go round, and the drive towards it is part of the human condition.

She is right to point out, however, that the ideal of celibacy, such a vital part of the priestly vocation, is given a woefully small part in seminary curriculae. The psychiatrist Dr Sipe writes that

'No seminary programme so far has solved the problem involved in inculcating celibate reality into the ministerial role.' In other words, it is something that must be taught and discussed.

Sister Mary, author of a collection of writings entitled *Celibate Loving*, believes in pushing the positive aspects, and suggests a self-help programme which includes making prayer-life paramount, and cultivating a 'rich, broad spectrum'[23] of non-sensual relationships.

Some religious orders have undertaken a radical overhaul of their recruitment procedures, in pursuit of positive celibacy. Sister Lavinia Byrne, who recently celebrated twenty-five years with the Institute of the Blessed Virgin Mary, has been closely involved in such reforms. Principal among them (and this idea is now being taken up by the Vatican) is the use of psychological screening procedures for candidates.

'It suggests to people firstly that we're interested in knowing them,' Sr Lavinia says, 'and secondly that we work with the real world. In religious orders, disclosure is now regarded as good. During noviciates, people are encouraged to be open about their sexual orientation, identity and experience. The old assumptions about every recruit being an eighteen-year-old virgin are no more. We try instead to provide an adjustmental context where people can sit back and look at themselves honestly. If they are going to make a vow of celibacy, then it has to stand the chance of being an authentic claim.'

At a time when female religious orders are finding it hard to maintain their numbers (only Mother Teresa's Missionaries of Charity are growing significantly) there is always a temptation to grab any potential recruit. 'But you do gain the best if you're honest,' Sr Lavinia says. 'And we have actually done better for recruits since we adopted this approach.'

Those fully prepared for the challenge of celibacy will be able to rise to it. For everything that he plans to renounce, Andrew Maggs at Wonersh has found compensation – even for the fact that he will never have a family. 'I know, God willing, that I won't become a father. But I have two nephew-cum-sons, and a niece-cum-daughter already. I can get things out of them that their parents don't. Christopher, my nephew, is Eurasian, and he wouldn't dream of talking to his mum and dad about the colour problems he's having at school. But I was at home one weekend, and we got into a long, long chat about colour problems. To see my own nephew trust me like that is one of the gifts I get.'

Fr McKay, however, doubts this is a substitute for true fatherhood. 'I'll never have children, and that is a great cross for me. I ache whenever I hold a baby at baptism. I've always felt that I'd make a good parent, but I'll never get the chance to find out.'

It is a poignant admission, and one that some of his parishioners may well find shocking. Alongside the liberal Catholics clamouring for change, there are always staunch traditionalists who simply cannot get their heads around the possibility of a priest having a sexual relationship. An Irish-born north London priest remembers an ecumenical experiment at his church, which involved a visit from the neighbouring Anglican vicar: 'I'm afraid some of my old dears couldn't cope with him at all. His talk went in one ear and out the other – they couldn't get over the fact that he was free to marry, and indulged in wild speculation about his relationship with his female parishioners. It was all the more embarrassing because the vicar in question was as camp as the proverbial row of tents. They'd have fallen off their chairs if I'd told them that.'

A parish priest's relationship with his parishioners is his stock in trade. He must address their problems in a responsible and caring fashion. And, inevitably, many of these problems are related to marriage. Catholics who have fallen foul of the Church's official line are now questioning the efficiency of counsellors who are celibate and male. Does their celibacy disqualify them from dishing out guidance to married couples?

No, according to some of Andrew's fellow-seminarians at Wonersh. They feel that to say a priest has to be married before he can counsel a couple is like saying a psychiatrist must have a breakdown before he can treat a patient. If a priest acts according to the Gospels and the Church, he will be doing his job.

Members of the Association of Separated and Divorced Catholics, a self-help group set up in 1981, reported mixed reactions from priests confronted with marital crises. As always, it is a case of selecting the right priest.

Sophie, an accountant from Middlesex, received very positive support from her priest. She had endured a violent, alcoholic husband for twenty years before turning in desperation to her parish priest when she and her children had been thrown out of their home. 'He was very sympathetic. He gave us a home in the presbytery for three months, while I went out to work in the City, to save for a mortgage.'

Other women in the group had darker tales to tell, of lectures about the sanctity of marriage, and advice to return to men who were beating them. The majority felt that there was little use in talking to a priest at all, because a man who was forced to be celibate himself was unlikely to sympathise with the problems of the married. With the Church piping one tune and the outside world another, it is difficult to hear those who sing the praises of the celibate state.

The Hireling Shepherd

> The good shepherd lays down his life for the sheep. The hired man, since he is not the shepherd and the sheep do not belong to him, abandons the sheep as soon as he sees a wolf coming.
>
> John 10:11–12

The Vatican loftily pretends not to see the sometimes unlovely oozings which appear when the crust of celibacy is broken. Several years ago, the US *National Catholic Reporter* printed a list of priests who had been involved in cases of child sex abuse. It filled several columns. In Canada, where the public health authorities and social services have been fighting a sustained campaign to uncover abuse of children, charges have been filed on 149 counts, against nineteen past and present members of the

Brothers of the Christian Schools. In Newfoundland, four Christian Brothers were convicted in 1991 of abuse at the Mount Cashel Orphanage. Ten diocesan priests have also been found guilty of similar offences, prompting the local archbishop, Alphonsus Penney of St John's, to resign after his handling of the affair was criticised.

Hubert O'Connor, former Bishop of Prince George diocese in central Canada, resigned in July 1991 after charges were pressed, alleging he had raped two women and indecently assaulted two others in the late 1960s, when he was principal of St Joseph's Mission School. In 1990, the school's supervisor, Fr Harold McIntee, was jailed for two years after admitting seventeen sex offences against young boys.

Canada is not a unique sink of priestly iniquity. Its honour roll of scandals is so long because the Canadian authorities are not shy about prosecuting priests and even bishops. The American Church is currently dealing with the scandal of Fr Dino Cinel, an Italian-born New Orleans priest who allegedly made pornographic videos of teenage boys in his rectory, and sold photographs of these boys to pornographic magazines. The devoutly Catholic District Attorney, Harry Connick, whipped up a storm of outrage when he admitted, in a television interview, that he had initially been unwilling to prosecute Cinel (despite recommendations from his investigators) because he did not wish to embarrass 'Holy Mother Church'. These days, Holy Mother Church cannot rely on such well-meaning, if wrong-headed, attempts to spare its blushes.[24]

Priests who commit acts of sexual abuse and violence have clearly traded on the trust inspired by their Roman collars – the trust in their celibacy – to exploit those weaker than themselves. As long ago as the twelfth century, St Bernard of Clairvaux was warning that the collective sex-drive of the Church, if deprived of honourable marriage, would burst out in all sorts of unspeakable directions. Being imprisoned by a vow of celibacy does not necessarily make a man a better shepherd. In some cases, he will be like the hireling of the Bible, forgetting all his responsibilities at the first sign of the wolf. So far, Rome has failed to address the role that enforced celibacy may have played in tne sexual crimes committed by priests.

Thankfully, the days when every priest caught cottaging was splashed all over the yellow press are almost gone. But a terrible fear of scandal and exposure is still keeping the old taboos in place. Driving the problem underground can, we believe, actually result in more scandals. It also places a priest – particularly a secular priest, isolated in his parish – under unbearable stress. There is a high rate of alcoholism among Catholic clergy. As the old saying goes, the two greatest dangers to a priest are the Punch and the Judy – drink and women.

Male and female created he them, and the God-given attraction between the sexes remains the main reason for broken vows among Catholic priests. They are forced into a heartbreaking choice between God and marriage. 'In my fourth year at the seminary,' recalls Fr Richard McKay, 'I met someone I liked a great deal and I started to think I might want to get married. But I knew I was called to be a priest, so eventually I decided to put all that aside and carry on with my studies.'

To avoid temptation, many priests try to cut themselves off from women altogether, thus exacerbating the marginalised position of Catholic women. From the seminary onwards, women are surgically removed from the lives of priests. Females allowed within the hallowed corridors will usually be nuns, who laid aside their sexuality when they made their vows.

This vetting procedure is not foolproof, because human nature will always out. 'It reminds me of the story of the old lady who had a beautiful cat,' says David, a thirty-year-old former seminarian. 'She was telling her neighbour how she wasn't going to let her cat have kittens when a randy tom came in. The neighbour pointed him out as a warning, and the old lady replied: "Don't worry, that's her brother."' Because priests are encouraged to be out of touch with their own sexuality, they will often kid themselves that a relationship with an attractive woman is purely pastoral.

Fr McKay again: 'Many priests have sublimated their feelings about sex. Too many Catholic priests are afraid of real human relationships. That's more or less how we're trained in the seminary, to be suspicious of any close friendships.'

To avoid the snares of female sexuality, the Church tends to apply the Augustinian method of painting every woman scarlet. Priests who do strike up close friendships with women – through working with them in a diocesan office, for example – are often marked men when it comes to promotion. Other priests, who are consulted when his name is put forward, will point the finger and say, 'He's very thick with so-and-so.' Enforced celibacy can turn good men into bigots, gossips and misogynists. The system is self-perpetuating, since it prevents those who might make changes from winning positions of power.

The situation is not helped by the women within the Church who feel that every female in the parish is a potential occasion of sin for Father, and that they should keep their distance.

In 1991, there was an illuminating correspondence in the *Tablet*, the London based international Catholic review. Representatives of the National Board of Catholic Women, an umbrella group of women's organisations in the Church, wrote in to urge more openness on this very issue. 'We know there are many good, loving relationships between women and priests – relationships which make a positive contribution to the life and work of both the priest and the woman. Yet, for the most part, these relationships remain secret and hidden. Jesus did not keep his friendships with women hidden.'[25]

Two weeks later came a response from four members of the Association of Catholic Women, an ultra-conservative group with strong grass-roots support in the parishes. They doubted that there were women who have secretly played 'affirming, loving and supporting' roles in the lives of celibate men, and demanded that any such should be named.

'It would be folly,' wrote these women, 'to suppose that all, or even most, close relationships between priests and women are spiritually helpful, especially if they are in close proximity in a "one-to-one" situation.' Referring to the previous letter's complaint about the 'secrecy, pain, rejection and abuse' women suffer as a result of sexual compromises with priests, the

Association of Catholic Women knew where they stood. 'Of course any woman who is, against her will, involved in a sexual relationship with a man deserves our sympathy. But what is the relevance here of clerical celibacy? Many would have thought that vows of celibacy would discourage such exploitation. Cases where priests have betrayed their trust with their female charges, or where nuns have exploited young males, are happily extremely rare.'[26]

The authors were unable to find any cases of nuns 'exploiting' young men. Cases of priests having affairs with women, however, are anything but rare. These well-meaning Catholic ladies have buried their heads in the sand: no, it just doesn't happen; and if it does, let's drum out the miscreants, and the wicked hussies who have led them astray. For them, any relationship between a woman and a priest can only mean one thing – sex.

'If they are talking about a mature woman who freely enters into a sexual relationship with a priest, on what grounds are we asked to sympathise with her? Or are we asked to believe, near the end of the twentieth century, that there are still women gullible enough to act on the assumption that a priest who is ready to break his promise of celibacy will nevertheless keep a promise of marriage?'[27]

As a matter of fact, as David Rice points out in his book, divorce among priests who have left to get married is amazingly rare, estimated at 5 per cent.[28] But the Association of Catholic Women would not wish to know about this statistic. As far as they are concerned, celibacy would be fine, if only naughty women didn't keep trying to spoil it.

However, the exploitation of women by priests is a very real problem, the ugliest skeleton in the Vatican closet. Not every priest who falls in love has the courage or the inclination to go public. When an elderly canon was buried in the north of England recently, the woman widely known as his 'wife' stood unacknowledged at his graveside.

The Church in Germany is trying to bring the sad condition of these 'wives' out into the open. In 1985, Ursula Goldmann-Posch published a book called *Unholy Alliances (Unheilige Ehen)*[29] which told the stories of priests and their forbidden sexual relationships.

When her husband died in 1982, Bettina was forty-five. They had heard Fr Michael speaking on the radio about death, and in her hour of need, she turned to him for support. An 'intense friendship' quickly grew up between them. Bettina felt a 'huge hunger for life, after this year of death. But I was very uncertain about the relationship, and certainly not the driving force that turned it into a love relationship. It was his initiative. I kept thinking "priests aren't allowed to do that." '

Three months after her husband's death, they had become lovers. 'And I noticed that he had only been waiting for me to say yes. He didn't need any more persuasion.'[30] Fr Michael, it turned out, was not a virgin. This was not his first lapse from his vows. After a great deal of pain and soulsearching, he decided to leave the priesthood. But Bettina insists that she put no pressure on him to do so. It was his decision.

Elizabeth, another of Goldmann-Posch's interviewees, met Fr Heinz in similar circumstances. Her husband had died and the priest was comforting her. She went to work for him, and a sexual relationship developed. When she discovered she was pregnant, she at first decided to have an abortion but could not go through with it.

During her pregnancy Fr Heinz kept his distance, fearful of causing a scandal in the small town where he worked. Elizabeth gave birth by caesarian, and spent four weeks in hospital. He did not visit her or their son, Markus, once. 'Fresh-cheeked fathers with roses and chocolates held their new children in their arms,' recalls Elizabeth. 'We were completely alone.' Fr Heinz was the hospital chaplain, and said he could not risk a visit.

Once she went home, he did begin to show an interest in his son. News of the 'problem' reached the ears of the local bishop, and one of his senior advisers visited the mother and child. He offered money and help, but on the condition that Elizabeth made no attempt to 'force' Fr Heinz to come and live with her. He left with the Christian benediction: 'May guilt haunt you.'[31]

David Rice quotes a letter from an American bishop to a priest who had resigned: 'if [. . .] you wish to return to the clerical state, you must leave your wife and children, if any, and obtain a civil divorce and do penance.'[32] In cases like these, the Catholic hierarchy has a heart of flint. And it directs its hostility at the women and children. If the erring priest admits he has been a bad boy and casts off his responsibilities, he will be welcomed back and no questions asked. Is a priest's celibacy really more important than the welfare of those he loves?

Alongside the priests who have been unable to keep their oaths of celibacy are those for whom the very sexlessness of the Church provides a safe hiding-place. It is a mistake to imagine that all vocations are made in heaven. The high proportion of homosexual priests (estimated at 33 per cent)[33] suggests that for some, the attractions of the priestly life are negative – an escape route from a sexuality they may not wish to confront.

'I remember reading a *Catholic Truth Society* pamphlet when I was young,' says David. 'It said that if you didn't feel attracted to girls, you had a vocation. And that was something I had been considering on and off since the age of fifteen. When I entered the noviciate at twenty-four, I still hadn't had any sexual experience. But at university, I'd been aware of the differences between me and my peer group. The way I built up friendships – or didn't – was different. I was always the one my male friends sent to comfort their girlfriends, when they had split up. And I'd go round, and often find myself lying on their beds, comforting those girls. But I didn't feel attracted to girls. I thought that if I was ordained, I would be valued as a counsellor. It's a service thing. I didn't have to evaluate my differences – just turn them into pluses by being a priest.'

David is now employed by a Catholic charity, having decided that the priestly role was not for him. Homosexuality, in itself, does not invalidate a vocation. There are many excellent priests who also happen to be gay. But David felt that his vocation had more to do with running away from that side of his nature.

Very few of the gay men we spoke to who had tested a vocation recall acknowledging their sexuality either publicly or privately when they entered seminaries. If they were running away from their sexuality, it was purely sub-conscious. James, now a writer in his forties is, however, an exception. 'I saw a vocation as a way of defeating my homosexuality and being comfortable with Christ. I felt as if the black hole into which I was falling was in check. It was as if I was too weak to survive in the world. And it worked. I didn't wank for a year. I was very into mortification of the flesh – rolling down hillsides in the snow, plunging my hands into boiling water. It was like an intense love affair with Christ. But it was not a mature view.'

James never even took the first set of vows required of a novice. His belief in his vocation ebbed as it failed to 'defeat' his homosexuality. After a sexual encounter with one of his tutors, he went over the wall.

Fr Paul, a parish priest in his forties, is happy to acknowledge his homosexuality, and has made the counselling of gay Catholics part of his ministry. Being gay, he says, has given him greater insight into why the priestly life is seen by some as a safe haven. 'You see so many priests who are uncomfortable with their sexuality. They don't like people getting close to them – they will only let them into the waiting room of the presbytery, and no further. They're the ones who are always seen buttoned up in their clerical black and Roman collars.'

The clerical costume sets a priest or nun apart. This is amplified in *Body and Soul*, a novel by Marcelle Bernstein about an enclosed nun who leaves her convent to care for her bereaved sister-in-law.

> She hadn't thought until now, when she was without it, that the habit had become a kind of costume, an identity she assumed each morning. It was in Bradford. She'd taken the boys to their nearby playground. It was cold and they had the place to themselves except for a young couple wrapped together on a bench, oblivious to everything. Seeing Anna in her grey cloak and head-dress, they had sprung apart, and sat shamefaced and giggling. Anna had been horrified by their response. They had seen only the message of her clothes; that she was against such expressions of life, of vitality, of sexuality.[34]

A distinction should be made here between those attracted to the priesthood as a means of escaping their sexuality, and those gay men motivated solely by a vocation. Like their heterosexual brothers, they can find the Church's enforced celibacy a bitter pill to swallow. For a gay priest, matters are further complicated by the Church's attitude to homosexuality – that it is a 'disordered' condition, inclining towards evil.

But does a homosexual relationship spoil a priest's ability to do the job? Fr John is a gay priest who has been involved in a steady relationship for three years. 'When I fell in love,' he says, 'I felt that my whole ministry burned with love. I was a better parish priest. I came alive. Officially, I'm committing a sin, but it doesn't feel like a sin – I have never felt so close to the Gospel's message of love.' Fr John's relationship is kept a deadly secret. He fears losing his parish if it came out in the open. He also fears having to choose between his lover and ministry, and privately fails to see why he cannot have both. 'The fact that the Church's attitude is to turn a blind eye whenever possible doesn't help.'

Sean, an Irish priest, had never acknowledged his homosexuality when he entered the seminary. A sexual advance from another man forced him to address the subject. When he turned to his seminary rector for guidance, he was sent to a psychiatrist. There was no discussion about how his discovery might affect his life as a priest – 'simply a trip to the shrink, and then silence'.

Damien, now in his late thirties and working for a Church organisation, was a student at Ushaw, the seminary of the northern English bishops. 'I was not fully identifying myself as a gay man when I went in. There was some wonderfully inept questioning from the Vocations Director – "Do you have a girlfriend?" I said no, but that I had friends who were girls. I thought it was what he wanted to hear, and because I wanted to get into the seminary, I was prepared to say it. On the selection panel was a woman introduced as the mother of five daughters. This was, I think, meant to make us feel comfortable. Someone with whom we might identify, rather like our own mothers. Well, bloody hell, if the woman has five daughters, she hadn't any experience of helping someone like me. I remember her asking if I had a girlfriend, and that was as far as it went.'

The blindness of seminary authorities to the fact of homosexuality can be astonishing, especially in seminaries where the number of homosexuals creates an overtly gay culture. 'I can remember the president [rector] at a college meeting,' says Damien, 'complaining about the increase in campery around the college. He said it wasn't an appropriate part of priestly lifestyle, and added that it was also insulting to genuine homosexuals – as if it was some sort of behaviour that affected straight men living together in college, rather than an acceptance that a high proportion of us were, in fact, gay.'

Not everyone is as short-sighted as the rector. In other quarters, there are fears that the overtly homosexual atmospheres in many of the seminaries are attracting too many gay men, and putting off heterosexuals. 'It is not inconceivable,' writes Richard P. McBrien, in the magazine *Commonweal*, 'that the ordained priesthood is attractive to certain people precisely because it excludes marriage. To put it plainly: as long as the Church requires celibacy for the ordained priesthood, the priesthood will always pose a particular attraction for gay men who are otherwise not drawn to ministry.'[35]

David Rice, quoting this passage in *Shattered Vows*, adds: 'In this regard I have in several places encountered a fear of what is called the "snowball effect" – young heterosexuals entering the seminary, and then being turned off by the gay culture they find there. So they quit, thus leaving the field to gays. And while a truly chaste homosexual ought not to be barred from ordination, a Church that became overwhelmingly homosexual in its clergy would hardly be acceptable to the heterosexual population.'[36]

The authors do not see why, if one is advocating a married priesthood, homosexual clergy need necessarily be 'truly chaste'. But the 'snowballing' of covert gays within the Church does have the unfortunate effect of deepening its hostility to women. 'I know it's not a fashionable thing to say, and doesn't sound at all liberal,' one feminist theologian told us, 'but there can be no doubt that homosexual cliques within the Church are keeping women out. It's the same in the Church of England – it's the gay cliques, hiding their sexuality under their clerical clothes, who are protesting the loudest about admitting women priests. They don't want girls in their cosy little club.'

The problem, as she sees it, stems from the enforced secrecy rather than the homosexuality. 'The Church's hostility to women always boils down to this basic hostility towards the sexual act itself. Many of these cliques believe that being homosexual is less sinful than fancying a woman. If only we could address the fact that we are sexual beings, the problem would not exist.'

David, the charity-worker quoted above, went on to teacher training college after leaving his seminary. 'In my teacher training, the thing they stressed was to remember how to fail. The teacher who forgets that is a bad teacher. But that is not what trainee priests were encouraged to do. So when things go wrong, priests often don't know what to do.'

Last year, a Belgian theologian accused the seminaries of institutionalising celibacy by not mentioning it; a process he described as 'tantamount to castration'. Some seminaries, however, influenced by progressives such as Sr Lavinia Byrne, are making changes. 'You can't, as a human being, be out of touch with sexuality,' says Mgr Peter Smith, the Rector of Wonersh. 'We have to understand it. As priests, we have to accept it, not deny it or repress it.'

Wonersh now attacks the issue head-on in its vetting procedures for potential recruits. It also runs a human development programme, in conjunction with a team of lay male and female psychologists and therapists. Sexuality is examined in the context of students' own experiences.

And Mgr Peter Smith insists that there is no turning of a blind eye. Students found having sexual relationships are, as a rule, asked to leave. In isolated cases, if he feels that there is no habitual pattern of such behaviour, Mgr Smith may give them a second chance provided the student takes the necessary steps to tackle the problem and resolve it. But he realises that to overlook sexuality altogether would be to 'plant a time-bomb' in the futures of his students.

This positive approach is still an exception rather than a rule. One priest responsible for addressing the topic of sexuality at an English seminary is less optimistic than Mgr Smith. Yes, he says, entry procedures are more thorough these days. But the use of psychological screening as advocated by the Vatican is, he claims, 'slanted at finding and rooting out the perverts'. And once a student gets into a seminary, the message is 'keep them in, whatever'.

'While the religious orders are reforming themselves, the diocesan seminaries seem to think that if you change the furniture to make the common room more hospitable, that's enough. They continue to prepare men for a life of renunciation, not interaction. If the Church makes sex into a bogey, it cannot then invite its seminarians to be in touch with it, to be honest.'

This priest runs optional workshops, on sexuality, towards the end of the seminarian's six years' training. 'Those who don't want to even begin to deal with it don't have to attend. Avoidance techniques are to the fore. It you took a random group of ten seminarians, four of them would probably say they were gay. Another group you will find over-represented in your random bunch are victims of childhood sex abuse. Having a vocation allows them to keep these things hidden. If I was cynical, I'd judge those vocations as avoidance.'

Religion and spirituality take the place of sexuality in cases like these, rather than combining with it to make a whole person. The more liberal-minded Church leaders feel that a gay priest who has come to terms with his sexuality is far better than one still cowering in the closet. As we have seen in an earlier chapter, there is a great deal of support for homosexuals in the British and American Churches. One senior English bishop has struggled for years with Rome, for the right to ordain avowedly gay men who are willing to live by the oath of celibacy. The question of their orientation is, he argues, irrelevant.

Many gay men become extremely successful parish priests, like Fr Paul. But Fr Paul feels he did all his learning about himself after he left the seminary. It has been a difficult process. Attempts to be honest with parishioners can misfire, because some people cannot bear to see their priest in any kind of sexual context. In one parish, Fr Paul tried to help a young man who came to him distraught, because he was gay. His offers of support were misinterpreted. He was reported to the bishop, and moved to the other side of the diocese, to assist an elderly, intensely homophobic canon.

By now, he feels that, through prayer and friendship, he has managed to reconcile his priesthood, his sexuality and his celibacy. So much so that he works to help others in similar situations. 'Since I began to get involved in gay issues, I have felt more in touch with myself. But at the same time, you realise the risks involved. If you do nothing as a gay man and a priest, that's fine by the Church. You're only in trouble when you're open. If I was dealing with my sexuality by furtively going off to a sauna which was known as a place where you could get cheap sex, then I'd be getting away with it, as far as the Church is concerned. But the fact that I am at peace with myself and try to help other people makes it all into a risk. That's the sad and absurd thing.'

Turning to other priests is an obvious help to those trying to cope with the high cost of mandatory celibacy. Recently, the Ministry to Priests programme has been heralded as a great source of mutual support – a kind of ecclesiastic Alcoholics Anonymous. But Fr Paul has found that such schemes in his area only perpetuate the dishonesty, and the terror of being found out.

'They don't deal with sexuality at all. There is so much fear surrounding the issue. Yet there is always going to be some risk involved in talking. Only then can you meet with other priests and discuss spirituality and sexuality. Everyone would have to accept that others may not be within the laws of the Church. If one priest admits to doing the gay club scene, it would do no good at all if the others were horrified. It's got to be a totally safe place. And at the moment, with so much fear among priests about sexuality, it just won't happen.'

Fr Sean, the Irish priest quoted above, has had painful experience of the Church's inability to cope with those who have failed to keep its rule of celibacy. He had struggled with his homosexuality in the seminary, but received no help. In his parish, he went through long periods of celibacy, but would occasionally seek the comfort of an anonymous sexual encounter with another man. He contracted the HIV virus. When he took the problem to his local bishop, he got a sympathetic hearing.

'He was fine, very understanding. Lots of tea and sympathy. I called a guy involved in the Ministry to Priests, and he said, you should definitely go on working. I said I didn't want to live with a priest in a parish where they didn't know my situation. I insisted that at least my colleague should know. Because if I'm whisked off to hospital and people come rushing in from the parish, they're going to know where I am – the AIDS ward. I don't want that. I want the initiative to come from me. Anyway, this guy was great. He said he knew lots of priests who would work with me under these conditions. And then the first guy he was "absolutely certain" of said no. He was too uncertain to call the rest.'

Sean was then passed on to the bishop in the next diocese, having been virtually abandoned by the Ministry to Priests co-ordinator in his own area. Once again, this man was initially helpful, but said he needed to bring the case before senior bishops. Despite all the promises, the bishop's plans to help Fr Sean were vetoed higher up. He was never told why.

'My bishop said he felt very bad that he'd led me on and raised my hopes. I said to him: "I'm not the first priest with HIV, and I won't be the last." The hidden message in my experience was "Don't tell us. We don't want to know."'

The Church's fear of departing from the ideals to address reality seems suicidal in cases like these. Priests with HIV or illegitimate children are embarrassments it does not know what to do with. They are stigmatised with the anathema of having broken their oaths of celibacy and indulged in sex. The top men in the Vatican must know, in their heart of hearts, that they are not 'special cases', but the tip of an iceberg – the ones who got caught. Instead of tackling the problems caused by enforced celibacy honestly, the Vatican tries to hide the evidence and pretend that the old rule is still working perfectly. When in Rome, try not to trip over the lumps in the carpets.

Five:
Whom God Has Joined

They are no longer two, therefore, but one flesh. So then,
what God has united, human beings must not divide.

MATT 19: 6

The word 'chastity' today, like 'virginity', 'purity' or
'modesty', has become abhorrent: even many who are
Catholic and want to be good do not aspire to be holy. They
may agree that adultery is wrong and intend to be faithful to
their husbands and wives, but they rebel against the idea that
there can be sexual sin within marriage, or that their fantasy
should be subject to moral law.

Piers Paul Read[1]

A woman can be proud and stiff
When on love intent;
But Love has pitched his mansion in
The place of excrement;
For nothing can be sole or whole
That has not been rent.

W. B. YEATS 'Crazy Jane Talks with the Bishop'

You stand together before the altar, and the priest blesses your
indissoluble union, making the two of you one flesh in the eyes of
God and Church. Congratulations – you have now achieved the
one state in which the Catholic Church permits sexual intercourse. From this moment, it will regard your couplings with a

127

benign smile instead of a disapproving frown. However, you should not imagine that you have left the sexual rules behind. You have merely exchanged one set for another.

To begin with, a lengthy section in the Code of Canon Law sets out who may and may not plight their troth in a Catholic church in the first place. These include people who have been baptised but not confirmed, those who are impotent, boys under sixteen and girls under fourteen, those who have not been baptised, and anyone who has murdered a former spouse.[2]

Strict enough rules, but as usual (except for the last) honoured as much in the breach as the observance. A sympathetic priest may relax the conditions of marriage so that, for instance, a devout member of his congregation can marry an avowed atheist in church. Choosing the right priest is vital.

Felicity, a convent-educated regular Mass attender, met and fell in love with a divorced man. Her parish priest refused to marry them (in fact, he gave her a lecture on renouncing the ways of the devil) and the couple ended up plighting their troth in a registry office.

Her friend, Vanessa, an outspoken atheist, was swept off her feet by a Catholic who attended Mass on average once a month. Six months later, they had a traditional church wedding. From the beginning, she had been honest about her lack of belief, and the fact that she had not been baptised, but this presented no problems to the priest.

When it comes to who qualifies for a church ceremony and who does not, the past and the future are taken into consideration. Felicity's problem was her partner's past. She had hoped that her priest would have taken a softer line – as he was fully empowered to do – and have overlooked the past in favour of the present. She came to understand the lottery system of the Church's attitude to divorce better when she moved to another parish, and found the young priest there only too happy to bless her marriage. Her problem had not been that she had fallen foul of Canon Law, but that she had not approached a sufficiently pliable priest.

A great deal depends on how an individual priest sees marriage

– as an indulgence, only grudgingly granted to people who have passed all the tests or as a symbol of love and commitment. The danger of the latter approach – as the authorities are continually warning priests – is that you can store up trouble for the future by being too relaxed in the present. The Code of Canon Law is full of references to the invalidity of marriages where certain conditions have not been met. If Felicity and her partner had married in church and subsequently split up, they would have a good case for an annulment. Annulment is the only kind of divorce available to practising Roman Catholics. Unlike civil divorce, which is based upon proofs of differences, annulment is based upon proofs that the marriage was invalid from the beginning, and therefore did not exist in the first place. If it did not exist, it cannot be said to have broken down. Ergo, Catholic marriages do not break down – QED.

Annulments are not easy to obtain. The Church likes its marriages to stick, hence the forest of official rules. Inevitably, these rules are enforced at the expense of personal compassion. In 1984, former soldier Stephen Rigby wanted to marry his fiancée, Ilona Bradhun, in a Catholic church. The Nottingham Diocesan Marriage Tribunal refused permission, because Rigby was paralysed and therefore judged to be impotent. The marriage would not be valid.[3]

The thought of a tribunal of professed Christians sitting around a table and coolly reducing the love between two people to a clause in Canon Law is amazing enough on its own, without even considering the Church's hardness of heart in actively discouraging this particular young couple's bid for happiness.

In the end, the local bishop intervened to enforce a loophole in the Code of Canon Law, which stated that if there was any future chance of a marriage being consummated it could be regarded as valid. Since the Church could not predict what science may make possible, Bishop James McGuinness ruled, the wedding could go ahead.

We do not think for a moment that the individuals judging the case were deliberately being unkind. But they seem to have been overwhelmingly conscious of the weight of the rule-book. They saw their responsibility in terms of riffling through that book for loopholes, instead of throwing it out of the window and following their hearts.

The case of Rigby and Bradhun reveals the official Catholic line on marriage in all its glory. It apparently has little to do with romance or love. Legally, it seems to be a chit you can exchange at approved outlets for sexual intercourse – a licence to fuck, along the lines of R. L. Stevenson's definition of marriage as a friendship recognised by the police.

Since marriage is the only state in which Catholics may have sex, the Church devotes a great deal of energy to deciding who qualifies. All around the world, there are literally thousands of priests in 'tribunals', poring over individual marriages to decide if they are now, have ever been or will ever be valid. And all of them are coming to different decisions. At meetings of the Association of Separated and Divorced Catholics, there are unofficial lists of the dioceses in England and Wales which have the most liberal tribunals – 'better to try for an annulment in Portsmouth rather than Newcastle', as one member put it. The ASDC is made up of devout Catholics, eager for the Church's approval, even if they have to get it on the black market.

'Marriage is something that needs to be very carefully regulated, to ensure the sanctity, the permanence of the bond,' a priest involved in one of these tribunals told us. 'The fussiness of the Church on validity dates from the time when people could get married under an apple tree, when there was no legal bond. In some countries, you can still get an annulment on the grounds that the witnesses were carrying side arms.'

Jonathan Swift, author of *Gulliver's Travels* and a Protestant clergyman, actually did marry a couple he met under a tree during a thunderstorm. The lines he scribbled for them as legal proof neatly encapsulate the Christian view of marriage:

> Under an oak, in stormy weather,
> I joined this rogue and whore together;
> And none but he who rules the thunder
> Can put this rogue and whore asunder.[4]

One Flesh

Christ may have been more reticent than the present-day Catholic Church would have liked on the subjects of masturbation, contraception and homosexuality, but he left us extremely emphatic views on the subject of marriage.

Christ approved of the married state, and judged it to be indissoluble. As we have said, this view flew in the face of Mosaic Law, which countenanced divorce.

> You have heard how it was said, You shall not
> commit adultery. But I say this to you, if a man looks at a
> woman lustfully, he has already committed adultery in his
> heart. [. . .]
>   It has also been said, Anyone who divorces his wife must
> give her a writ of dismissal. But I say to you, everyone who
> divorces his wife, except for the case of an illicit marriage,
> makes her an adulteress; and anyone who marries a divorced
> woman commits adultery.
>
> MATT 5: 27–28, 31–32

(By 'illicit marriage', Christ means a marriage within the Jewish forbidden degrees – near enough the ancient equivalent of a registry office wedding.) The sanctity of the eternal bond of Christian marriage comes, therefore, from no less a person than the Son of God himself. The authors (one of whom is married) hold true to this as an ideal. We feel that for those who believe in God, it is impossible to get married in a Church more than once. The marriage service is a binding vow you make with one person, before the throne of heaven. You cannot turn up before the same throne a few years later, expecting to make the same vows with someone entirely different – excuse me God, slight mistake, could you forget the eternal vows I made last time?

We also accept, however, the reality that marriages do break down. And since we have never met anyone who got divorced for fun, or found the process enjoyable, we believe that divorces

131

should be made as painless as possible both by the State and the Church. Condemning those who have already suffered the pain of an unhappy marriage is pointlessly cruel. So is refusing them the possibility of blessedness in a subsequent relationship. The Church is following Christ in blessing second partnerships. As one priest, who does his best to welcome couples officially living in sin, puts it: 'Are we Christians, or are we a bunch of farts?' Compassion is a Christian's business. It is not up to us to condemn those who have fallen short of Christ's ideals.

These ideals, as stated in the Gospels, do not include any sexual restrictions within marriage. Christ was anything but a killjoy – at the wedding he attended at Cana (John 2), where he changed the water into wine, there is no record of him delivering a Catholic homily about sex being purely for procreation. Never once did Christ put forward this view. Instead, he emphasised the bond that should exist between a married couple – physical as well as spiritual.

> He answered, 'Have you not read that the Creator from the beginning made them male and female, and that he said: This is why a man leaves his father and mother and becomes attached to his wife, and the two become one flesh? They are no longer two, therefore, but one flesh. So then, what God has united, human beings must not divide.'
>
> MATT 19: 4–6

St Paul, though less positive about marriage as opposed to virginity, also wrote of a bond of flesh.

> Husbands must love their wives as they love their own bodies; for a man to love his wife is to love himself. A man never hates his own body, but feeds it and looks after it.
>
> EPHESIANS 5: 28–29

He precedes this advice by telling women they must be 'subject to their husbands as to the Lord, since, as Christ is head of the

Church and saves the whole body, so is a husband the head of his wife' (Eph 5: 22–23). Here is yet more source-material for those seeking the roots of the Catholic Church's appalling misogyny, and it's a depressing assumption that the female's role in marriage is that of a domestic servant. Feminist theologians, however, have fastened on verse 21 in the same chapter of the letter: 'Be subject to one another out of reverence for Christ.' And in his Letter to the Galatians, St Paul writes: 'There can be neither Jew nor Greek, there can be neither slave nor freeman, there can be neither male nor female – for you are all one in Christ Jesus' (Gal 3: 28). Clearly, unlike later saints, St Paul did not dismiss women as spiritually inferior. Neither did he mention such a thing as sexual sin within marriage. How can one flesh sin against itself?

Over the next four centuries, as Gnostic influences bled into early Christianity, the sacred bond of marriage began to be seen as inferior to the blessed wholeness and purity of virginity. Around AD 390, a monk named Jovinian suggested that virginity was not, in fact, better than marriage. This view so angered St Jerome that he wrote '*Adversus Jovinian*', a violently anti-feminine, anti-sex reply: 'The distance between marriage and virginity is the distance between avoiding sin and doing good [. . .] Marriage fills the earth, virginity fills heaven.'[5]

In his turn, possibly feeling that Jerome was veering dangerously towards the Manichean view of marriage as evil, St Augustine wrote '*De Bono Conjugali*' (Of Good Marriage). St Augustine felt that marriage, as ordained by God, had a use in populating the earth. His tract is, however, hardly an advertisement for the married state. 'If a man were weary of being alone,' he says, 'how much more suited for common life and good conversations would have been two male friends living together than a man and a woman.' St Augustine does not think companionship between male and female can have been part of the Lord's plan for us. He takes Christ's phrase 'one flesh' as an allusion to the formation of Eve from Adam's rib. Already, Christ's ideal is beginning to sour.

Peter Damian, an eleventh-century theologian and lawyer who was to influence St Thomas Aquinas, believed that neither

Mary nor Joseph had ever had sexual intercourse, and that Jesus entered the world without breaking his virgin mother's hymen. 'One sees him coming ever nearer to [. . .] the old Gnostic dualist doctrine,' writes the Cambridge Professor Christopher Brooke, 'that the material world is wholly evil, even its creation; that the only hope of good in this life is to escape from the flesh into the spirit [. . .] Damian and all known theologians before Abelard, and most before the great thirteenth-century scholastics, took it for granted that the act of the marriage-bed was only just and righteous if the parties took no pleasure in it.'[6]

St Thomas Aquinas, in his *Summa Theologiae*, pointed out that virginity without spirituality must not be elevated too highly: 'martyrs cleave to God more mightily, because they lay down their own lives, whilst those who dwell in monasteries lay down their own wills and all they possess; virgins lay down only the pleasures of sex.'[7] Linked to theological virtue, however, he found virginity superior, even to a 'continent' marriage.

In the first centuries after Christ, then, even sex within marriage came to be considered sinful. Men and women who refused to consummate their unions were considered virtuous. St Etheldreda, in seventh-century England, went through two marriages without losing her virginity. The medieval Church forbade sexual intercourse between married people during Lent, and on feast days and Sundays. Here are the roots of the modern Church's reluctance to get out of Catholic bedrooms. Sex is a sin. Lust remains evil, even when wearing a wedding ring. The faithful must be prevented from sinning.

The Second Vatican Council, in the encyclical *Gaudium et Spes*, dramatically blew away the cobwebs by emphasising the love within marriage, and admitting that married sex had other functions besides the begetting of children: 'a free and mutual giving of self, experienced in tenderness [. . .] a far cry from mere erotic attraction, which is pursued in selfishness and soon fades away in wretchedness [. . .] Even in cases where despite the intense desire of the spouses there are no children, marriage still retains its character of being a whole manner and communion of life.'[8]

Since the 1960s, the Vatican has taken pains to relate every aspect of marriage to its most sacred totem, the family. 'The family,' says *Gaudium et Spes*, 'is the place where different generations come together and help one another to grow wiser and harmonise the rights of individuals with other demands of social life; as such it constitutes the basis of society.'[9]

Collectively, the Catholic Church tends to concentrate its efforts on areas it perceives to be under threat. In late twentieth-century society, divorce and single parenthood are shattering the stereotype of the family unit. Worse, thanks to Sigmund Freud and his successors, that unit is increasingly seen as a battleground, the source of all our neuroses. But it is very much in the Church's interest to keep the hierarchy of the family in place – especially the mother, who is usually responsible for bringing little Catholics into the fold. 'Traditionally, there has been no concept of love at the centre of a marriage,' says Sister Myra Poole. 'A woman was simply the chattel of her husband. The Catholic Church reinforced this by only ever viewing women as wives and mothers.'

The family still held up as the model is the Holy Family. And it is an odd model – a couple who apparently never had sexual intercourse, bringing up a child conceived out of wedlock, albeit by the Holy Spirit. The 'brothers and sisters' of Jesus are mentioned several times in the Gospels, yet theologians have variously explained them away as cousins, or St Joseph's children by a previous marriage. St Matthew's Gospel states that Joseph did not have sex with Mary before the birth of Jesus: 'he had not had intercourse with her when she gave birth to a son,' as the New Jerusalem Bible translates it (Matt 1: 25). The King James Bible puts a slightly different slant on the same verse: 'And knew her not till she had brought forth her firstborn.' The single word 'till' implies that Joseph 'knew' his wife after Jesus' birth. The Catholic removal of that little word perpetuates the legend that the marriage of Mary and Joseph was sexless.

The balance of power within a family, the forcing of its members into assigned roles, has become as important to the Church as carefully regulated sex between the parents. The ideal family mirrors the Thatcherite ideal, in which men must work and women must weep, when there's little to earn and many to keep. Father going out to work and mother minding the brood at home is still seen by many as the cure for all society's ills. Yet again, however, anyone with eyes in their head can see that the ideal conflicts with the reality. It is not a question of 'allowing' the traditional family unit to break down – the rising number of children in single-parent families shows that it already has broken down. And where pressure is put upon people to stay within the framework, the results are not necessarily happy.

'The Irish capacity for domestic unhappiness has suffered greatly in the process,' says the Irish writer Frank Delaney. 'The attitude to sex stood for barbarism in familial conduct, for bitterness, for lack of charity, for malice.' When the family must be upheld at all costs, the Catholic Church has a fine record of ignoring battered wives and abused children, because acknowledging that such things occur within the sacred unit would mean admitting that it was less than perfect.

For the same reasons, the Catholic Church is uncomfortable with women who have broken away from their traditional family role, and particularly uncomfortable with those who have achieved any kind of eminence in the Church. Kathleen O'Gorman, director of Westminster Diocesan Education Service, is vilified by priests more than any man doing the same job in other parts of the country. Jean Judge, the liberal-minded chief executive of the Catholic Marriage Advisory Council, is another favourite Aunt Sally. Priests have often complained that she is not Catholic enough in her approach. Oh, the pity of it all – that the conspiracy to make the Catholic Church look ridiculous should come from within its own ranks.

The ideal of the family continues to exert a powerful attraction. Parents are queuing to send their young to Catholic schools, even those who have had bad experiences at the hands of monks and nuns. Good exam results and 'discipline' act as magnets. Having school-age children can often draw a lapsed couple back to church, because Mass attendance is stipulated by the governors of many Catholic schools. We are back to priest power again.

Vatican Roulette

The greatest power the Church has over a devout married couple, however, is its continued insistence that the sexual act must always have the possibility of conception. As we have seen, this was modified in the 1950s by the introduction of 'natural' family planning. Couples wishing to space their children must make love only during the 'safe' period of a woman's menstrual cycle, when conception is least likely to occur. Increased moisture in the vagina and a rise in temperature just before ovulation warn the woman to abstain from sex. 'It is good that women know about their bodies,' enthuses Mary Kenny, 'that they are not afraid to look at their moisture levels, at their vaginas, and that men get involved so that they are not afraid of sex and reproduction.'

Her less traditional opponents would point out that, far from reducing fear, this process increases it, surrounding the whole business of sex with anxiety. David Lodge, in his early novel *The British Museum is Falling Down*, got considerable comic mileage out of Natural Family Planning, describing the young wife's morning ritual of sticking a thermometer in at either end. But the reality of Vatican Roulette can be anything but amusing. Helen, a forty-five-year-old divorcee, maintains that 'being told to use the rhythm method is a very bad start to marriage. When your relationship's having problems, you can't just kiss and make up, using sex as an expression of love, because you've got three kids already and you don't want a fourth.'

US writer Mitch Finley, co-author with his wife Kathy of *Christian Families in the Real World*, believes that NFP causes unnecessary stress in modern Catholic marriages. 'Under most circumstances,' he writes, 'in a healthy marriage making love is the most complete way husband and wife can ritualise and revitalise their love. Indeed, one may say that when spouses make love they celebrate in a special way the sacrament of marriage. Ordinarily, couples should no more welcome the chance to avoid loving sexual intercourse than they would rejoice at the opportunity to miss Mass on Sunday.'[10]

Finley blends his religious devotion with a strong sense of practicality, and his argument will strike chords with many Catholic couples. 'What healthy Catholic marriages need is a safe family planning method that enables them to space and limit pregnancies responsibly, one that also allows them to make love frequently, and when the Holy Spirit moves them.'[11]

Fundamentalists hold up their hands in horror at the idea that it is the Holy Spirit which moves people to have sexual intercourse – no wonder, when all the Church's teachings since Augustine have held that lust is the work of Satan. We also sense a reluctance to allow people the freedom to decide how many children they have. Suppose they stop after one? Suppose they decide to have none? Better not to let them have the choice in the first place.

From the Church's point of view, the great boon of NFP is its rate of failure. Finley cites Dr John Queenan, head of obstetrics and gynaecology at Georgetown Medical School, USA, who reports that pregnancy rates among those using NFP range from eleven to twenty per cent. Fr Sean McDonagh, an Irish missionary working in the Philippines, tells us that: 'in eight years, not a single family, not even those in daily contact with the sister nurse, has been able to apply these methods successfully.' One member of the Association of Separated and Divorced Catholics says: 'when I told my priest, before marriage, that I wanted children as soon as possible, he told me to use the rhythm method.'

Somewhat confusingly, given the reputation of NFP for achieving the precise opposite of what it sets out to do, World Health Organisation figures show its failure rate as no higher than other 'artificial' methods. To square this circle requires a variation on our running theme of the ideal and reality. In a perfect world, say the Family Planning Association, NFP is very safe. By ideal they mean where women have monthly cycles as regular as clockwork and where they dedicate their lives to monitoring the minute variations in their temperature and vaginal mucus.

'Today NFP is becoming fashionable again as a green, trendy

thing to do,' says the FPA. 'It's natural and there are no messy disposables to clutter up the environment. But your commitment to it must be complete if it is going to succeed. You must always take your temperature as soon as you wake up, whatever other calls nature is making. You have to be aware that even an Aspirin could cause a temperature fluctuation and be prepared not to have sex for a considerable part of each month.'

A healthy and spiritual discipline, the bods in the Vatican would claim, putting sex on a pedestal. Impossible, say the people in the pews. Our lives are not as regimented. As one NFP instructor told us: 'There's nothing wrong with the method in theory. It's the people who are the problem.'

As a method of contraception, Vatican Roulette plainly will not do. While some devout Catholics struggle with temperature charts and periods of abstinence, others – equally devout – are quietly using artificial methods. The majority of married people we spoke to felt free to ignore *Humanae Vitae*. These days, only ultra-traditionals, such as the writer Piers Paul Read quoted at the beginning of this chapter, think that chastity within marriage has anything to do with holiness.

Assisted Procreation

> And [Hannah] vowed a vow, and said, O Lord of hosts, if thou wilt indeed look on the affliction of thine handmaid, and remember me, and not forget thine handmaid, but wilt give unto thine handmaid a man child, then I will give him unto the Lord all the days of his life.
>
> 1 SAMUEL 1: 11[12]

The pleadings of the Old Testament heroine, Hannah, poignantly illustrate the grief of childlessness. It has been estimated that approximately one in ten couples will have difficulty conceiving. In Hannah's day, prayer was the only hope. Christians will naturally insist that prayer still helps, but modern technology has come up with various artificial methods of assisting conception. These include IVF (*in vitro* fertilisation), in which the sperm and the ovum are fertilised outside the mother's body and implanted in her womb; and the artificial insemination of the mother with the semen of a man other than the father.

These scientific advances have been a blessing to many couples, but they have caused some sleepless nights among the law-givers of the Vatican. Yes, the primary purpose of marriage is the begetting of children. But the separation of the sexual act from the procreative is contrary to Catholic doctrine. In 1987, the Congregation of the Doctrine of the Faith, under the eye of its prefect, Cardinal Ratzinger, produced '*Donum Vitae*', the official Roman line on reproductive technology.

'*Donum Vitae*' is not calculated to make any childless Catholic couple feel more hopeful. The Vatican's principal objection to IVF is, predictably, that more than one egg at a time is fertilised outside the body, and that these embryos may subsequently be destroyed or even used for experiments. This contradicts the Church's teachings on the dignity of human life from the first moment of conception, and belongs under the heading of abortion.

The second objection, however, is that artificial insemination and IVF, like contraception, separate the sexual act from its sole procreative purpose. 'Contraception deliberately deprives the conjugal act of its openness to procreation and in this way brings about a voluntary dissociation of the ends of marriage. Homologous artificial fertilisation, in seeking a procreation which is not the fruit of a specific act of conjugal union, objectively effects an analogous separation between the goods and the meanings of marriage. Thus, fertilisation is licitly sought when it is the result of a conjugal act which is *per se* suitable for the generation of children to which marriage is ordered by its nature and by which the spouses become one flesh. But from the moral point of view procreation is deprived of its proper perfection when it is not desired as the fruit of the conjugal act.'[13]

You could be forgiven for thinking that the Catholic Church would be delighted by any method of procreation which did not involve the sin of sexual desire. But no. The mere idea that sex can be seen as separate from reproduction is anathema.

'Artificial insemination as a substitute for the conjugal act,' declares '*Donum Vitae*', 'is prohibited by reason of the voluntarily achieved dissociation of the two meanings of the conjugal act. Masturbation, through which the sperm is normally obtained, is another sign of this dissociation.' Well, we might have guessed. 'Even when it is done for the purpose of procreation, the act remains deprived of its unitive meaning: It lacks the sexual relationship called for by the moral order.'[14]

This argument is not universally accepted within the Church. The Jesuit writer William Daniel feels the Vatican has got its logical and moral wires crossed. 'What does this tell us,' he asks, 'about the necessity of achieving procreation within the sexual act? One could say likewise that the dignity of human eating, the ritual and the spiritual refreshment of the meal, the notion that our eating should not just be the ingesting of the food in a merely animal fashion, is all based on the unity of the soul and body in the human being [. . .] Tube feeding of a comatose patient has little of these spiritual qualities, and this is indeed a loss; but this does not make tube feeding of the comatose immoral.' Ingeniously, Daniel adds: 'What would be immoral would be to set up tube feeding for a busy Ph.D. student so that his hands would be free for the keyboard of his computer.'[15] It would be wrong to have IVF for the sake of convenience, but not out of necessity.

Liberals in Catholic ranks cling to the fact that '*Donum Vitae*' 'allows' a technique called GIFT. This acronym, which has an attractive ring in the context of conception, translates with a disappointingly unpoetic precision as 'gametes intra-fallopian transfer'. And the truth of the situation is that the rule-book – in this case '*Donum Vitae*' – makes no mention at all of GIFT. Silence is taken by liberals to be consent.

A more likely explanation for its inhibition is that Rome has been unable to pin down quite what GIFT is. Some specialists who claim to be using GIFT offer techniques that are simply IVF by another name. Some, however, take GIFT to mean the transfer of an egg from the ovary to the lower end of the fallopian tube to overcome a blockage – and then conception takes place in the usual, or as the Vatican would say, the natural way. This version, giving God a helping hand, gets the green light from papal advisers.

They are rather more dubious on an adaptation that doctors say gives God a sporting chance. GIFT Mark Two again involves transferring the egg down the fallopian tube but this time round it is artificially fertilised inside the body. Not quite IVF in that there are no test-tubes involved, but there is that tricky question of how you collect the sperm.

Here, the specialists have come up with an ingenious way of shortcircuiting Rome's objections. Have sex but use a condom with a small hole in. And then let the doctors do their bit. The theory goes that you will never know how the baby came about. It might just have been in the natural way. The medics aren't fooled and neither are the couples involved. But Rome is happy.

Yes, it is complicated stuff; a real theological granny-knot, accompanied by the age-old metaphysical sounds of angels' feet frolicking on the heads of pins. The Church also seems to be anxious about the banishing of God to a mere supporting role in AI and IVF: 'Homologous IVF and ET [Embryo Transfer] is brought about outside the bodies of the couple through actions of third parties whose competence and technical activity determine the success of the procedure. Such fertilization entrusts the life and identity of the embryo into the power of doctors and biologists and establishes the domination of technology over the origin and destiny of the human person.'[16]

We would suggest that God, being all-powerful, cannot be threatened by the actions of his created beings. Science and technology are not things apart from God, and can often be used according to his will.

There is much to be said for '*Donum Vitae*'s upholding of human dignity, and its insistence that the Church has a duty to guard respect for human life. Quite rightly, the document points out that 'marriage does not confer upon the spouses the right to have a child'.[17] To suppose that children are a 'right' is to equate them with chattels.

But *'Donum Vitae'* is very cold comfort indeed for Catholic couples having problems with fertility. IVF is a complicated, traumatic process, with a low rate of success. It is usually a childless couple's last hope. We do not feel the Church has a right to increase their anxiety and suffering by condemning their last hope of becoming parents.

And neither, it seems, do many Catholics desperate for children. Some call their chosen technique GIFT and take comfort in the fact that they are not officially condemned. Others, already bemused by science, leave theological niceties to the theologians and make a pragmatic choice for the procedure with the best track record, IVF. Mark, our Benedictine-educated journalist, and his wife were keen to start a family but several years passed without success. They discussed artificial techniques. Despite Mark's earlier endorsement of the papal line in documents like *Humanae Vitae* about the sanctity of life, they decided they had no objections to IVF. 'It depends if you see human life as accidental. God says in the Bible, speaking of Israel but it applies to us as well, "before you were formed in the womb, I knew you". There can be no accidents in birth. It's not something we work out. It was intended before we were born.'

In the end the couple were among the lucky ones and managed by natural means to have a baby. For those less fortunate the same church that upholds the ideal of the family as something that no one can be complete without, remains tied to its cruel and unbending rule-book. As Frances Kissling of Catholics for a Free Choice puts it: 'instead of telling us to transcend our bodies in sex as they usually do, they say that a loved child can only be created by the sex act. Love therefore equals genital sexuality. Only a penis in a vagina means love.'

Human Beings Must Not Divide

Beyond the question of the Church's sexual rules for married people lies the question of what it offers to those whose marriages have broken down. Between 1960 and 1987, the number of divorces in England and Wales increased sixfold. Around one in three marriages are biting the dust.[18]

And despite the claims of certain stubborn priests, there is no evidence that these are only non-Catholic marriages. Faced with such widespread rejection of the Christian ideal of marriage, the Church has tried to push the advantages and joys. More practically, it has also tried to make its pre-nuptial counselling more realistic and more thorough. Many people still yearn for a traditional white wedding at the altar, and that gives the Church a responsibility (and an excellent opportunity) to put across the meaning of the marriage service. The process has recently moved away from a single chat with a red-faced priest to elaborate residential courses for engaged couples, and sessions with young marrieds in the parish to talk frankly about the challenges ahead. There has been a proliferation of preparation books – such as the one for non-believers, snappily entitled: *So You're Marrying a Catholic.*

At parish level, it has been accepted that a celibate priest does not have all the answers, and that those who are married themselves have most to offer. The marriage preparation is not exactly optional – you may have the right to refuse it, but don't forget, the priest has a right to refuse you your white wedding.

Vanessa and her partner were less than happy at having to wait six months to ensure that their commitment was genuine when the priest knew they were living together – sign enough of their commitment, they felt. But Vanessa, who went through the preparatory course so that her partner could have the church wedding he wanted, found herself enjoying some of their sessions with a local Catholic couple. Throughout the whole exercise, however, she saw an irritating tendency to deafness whenever she mentioned that she did not actually believe in God.

Jenny, a convent-educated lawyer in her thirties, wanted to marry in her parents' parish church, and had to go on a residential weekend course before the priest would agree. 'Jack, my husband, has no religious beliefs, but he was the one who took the weekend seriously. I felt that among the Catholics in our group, there was a sense of resignation, of letting what was being said wash over us, as it had in the classroom. The non-Catholics kept challenging the priest who talked to us. When he said how marvellous marriage was, Jack stopped him and said, "How do you know?" And the priest didn't have any real answer. It didn't make Jack respect the Catholic Church.'

The involvement of a priest at such weekends is not statutory, and increasingly less common. The role of the professional religious has changed since the days when Daniela, now in her fifties, went for her pre-marital homily. 'A nun gave us tips on how not to fall out – like always putting the top back on the toothpaste. Sex was not, of course, mentioned.'

When a marriage runs into trouble, though the priest may be the first port of call in the storm, most are now admitting their limitations, and directing couples to the local Catholic Marriage Advisory Council. These groups, which also work with engaged couples, are funded both by the bishops and the Home Office. Their approach offers a beacon of hope for those liberal Catholics who are urging the Church to take more notice of the reality of peoples' lives, instead of clinging blindly to an ideal.

Jean Judge, the chief executive of the CMAC in England and Wales, does not wish her organisation to be seen as an arm of the Vatican, only peddling the line that marriage is for life. 'We know from experience that many people avoid seeking our help because of the word "Catholic" in our title. I am under consider-able pressure to remove it. The public image of the Church, particularly in the area of sex and sexuality, is not good. The Church is, for many, rigid, intolerant, judgemental and punitive.'

A truly Catholic approach to marital difficulties, Mrs Judge believes, lies in helping and supporting people whatever their circumstances. 'One aspect that is understood is forgiveness. People know they can turn to the Church for forgiveness, but they also know that forgiveness depends on a firm purpose of amendment. This is often a condition they can't meet. What they are looking for, and what they need, is acceptance. This can be hard for the Catholic Church to give, because we can appear to be condoning. By offering acceptance, we believe that we get as near as possible to the unconditional love of God.'[19]

The conservatives' fear of appearing to 'condone' can outweigh their wish to 'accept'. Many Catholics whose marriages have broken down are left only with a sense that they have failed, and that the Church is turning its back on them because of it. Pat, an Irish-born nurse, married the first man who happened along. 'I was brought up to believe in the sanctity of marriage, and had a highly romanticised view of married life. When my marriage began to go wrong, I could only assume it was because I was doing something wrong.' Her guilt made her stay away from the Church. Without any support she struggled on, until the day her husband beat her up so badly that she fled to a women's refuge.

Traditionally raised Catholics often believe that they have a duty to persevere in a failed marriage, come what may. 'Our marriage really ended after ten years,' says Sandra, from London's Italian community. 'I was thirty-one and he gave me gonorrhoea. He told me he caught it from eating chickens. He swore on his mother's life. When I was lying in hospital, I thought, God, I don't deserve this one! But I also thought, Stephano's done something so awful to me that now he'll have to treat me better. But he didn't.' In her despair, Sandra began attending a church run by some missionary priests, who were so welcoming that she poured out her troubles. They supported her in her decision to leave her husband.

The kind of sticking power displayed by Sandra is one of the classic virtues of the traditional Catholic wife. Men may drink and abuse and sleep around, but the woman must keep home and family together at all costs. 'The Church taught me to believe that marriage meant always putting my husband first,' says Daniela, 'and that child-bearing was my main function in life. I never questioned this. The Church's view of women and the wording of the Catholic marriage ceremony gave my husband a warped view of my role. He interpreted my promise to obey him as meaning to put up with a stream of affairs, violence, and a complete lack of interest in our children.'

The extent to which the Church, with its insistence that

marriages are made in heaven, has oppressed women was acknowledged by Canada's bishops in 1991, in their statement 'To Live Without Fear'.[20] In their guidelines for priests dealing with broken marriages, they admitted past errors in sending abused women back to their husbands: 'Counselling premature reconciliation will not stop the abuse, protect the woman or provide any healing. In an abusive situation, the priority must be the safety of the woman. This may involve a marital separation.'

It is not enough, say the bishops, to make a purely private commitment to these people. The Church must show public support. 'The abused woman is often very isolated. Church may be the one place she is still able to go. If she never hears a homily on this topic, her sense of isolation may be increased or she may not feel free to approach her pastor or a member of the pastoral team.'[21]

In Britain, where bishops have been more reluctant to admit officially that some separations should be backed by the Church, the Association of Separated and Divorced Catholics has flourished. Founded in 1981, the ASDC is both a self-help group and a pressure group which lobbies for greater acceptance by the Church. The results have been spectacular. ASDC branches have sprung up all over the country, and bishops have publicly announced concern for the divorced. Cardinal Hume celebrated the Association's tenth anniversary Mass at Westminster Cathedral.

But ten years is the blink of an eye against nearly two thousand years of tradition and teaching, and divorced Catholics may still experience prejudice and condemnation out of all proportion to their 'crime'. In 1990, Hans Formella was appointed head of St Oswald's Catholic Primary School in Richmond, West London. The choice was not popular with the Archdiocese of Southwark, which has a controlling majority on the board of school governors. Mr Formella was divorced. Worse, he had remarried without having had his first marriage annulled. In the eyes of the Catholic Church, and certainly in the eyes of the Archdiocese, he was living in sin, and unfit for a position of authority in a Catholic school. When governors protested that Formella was a good teacher and a devout man, whose personal problems had not been of his own making, they were sacked.[22]

Possibly, if Formella had merely been divorced, the Archdiocese might have turned a blind eye. And possibly, he might have got away with merely living with his second wife. But he was ruled out because his secular marriage would bring the teaching of the Church into disrepute. It could not countenance such a public flouting of the rules.

The Ecclesiastical Alternative

In 1989, the Church that stands so staunchly for the sanctity of marriage annulled 54,736 Catholic unions.[23] The lengthy process of annulment can happen without the co-operation of the former spouse, but it drags on for ages – often years after a civil divorce has gone through. An annulment is vital for Catholics who wish to remarry in church. Every sexual act they commit before annulment is adultery in the eyes of the Church.

Annulment is not a soft option. Intimate details of your sex life will be pored over and minutely discussed by two diocesan tribunals, in search of reasons why the marriage could be declared null and void. The first tribunal examines the nuts and bolts, questioning relatives, friends and anyone who can give evidence about the nature of the relationship. The second tribunal scrutinises the findings of the first. Usually, this is a rubber-stamp job, but if the second tribunal disagrees, it can send the case off to yet another desk in Rome.

In theory, the criteria are strict. The marriage can be declared invalid if any of the rules laid down in Canon Law have been broken – even with the knowledge of the priest concerned. 94 per cent of the 1989 annulments were granted on the grounds of invalid consent by one or other of the partners. This covers a whole range of excuses, including one or both partners being emotionally immature or not making their vows sincerely.

Just 138 of those annulments were granted on the grounds of

impotence. Interestingly, 64 were in Poland. We suspect that this has less to do with the debilitating effects of red cabbage and vodka than the vagaries of different national annulment tribunals. Attitudes across the world, and even from one diocese to another, vary widely. 84 per cent of those 1989 annulments were granted in the Americas.[24]

Experiences of annulment can be extremely diverse. At one gathering of a London branch of the ASDC, we saw the room dividing between those who felt it was a positive course of action, and those who felt it had been a humiliating invasion of their privacy. One woman described the questions asked on the annulment form as 'tantamount to rape'. One of the men told us that giving evidence to the tribunal was 'like spending three hours in the confessional'.

It must be said, however, that people from other Christian communions sometimes envy Roman Catholics for having the option of a divorce that is granted by the Church authorities. The Protestant attitude to divorce and remarriage is far more relaxed at most levels – few Anglicans fall foul of their priests for living in sin – but you only get one shot.

In Ireland, one of the few states where divorce is not allowed, annulment is the only option. The Irish situation is complicated and peculiar. A referendum on divorce in the mid-1980s produced a big No vote. The outcome of the ballot was strongly influenced by the Catholic Church, which fought a vigorous anti-divorce campaign from the pulpits. The paradox is that the same Church allows annulment. So the Irish can annul their failed marriages before the Church, but not before the state, because the Church won't let it.

'One of the great hypocrisies in Ireland is the matter of annulment,' declares Frank Delaney, whose divorce made headlines in Ireland (people still cross the street rather than speak to him as a result). 'When I was in my teens, there was no such thing as divorce, separation or anything legally recognised in society, because the Church said no. But if you had the money, you could buy an annulment. A businessman once told me he paid £5000 to the Church in Dublin.'

Throwing money at the problem does not always work. One of the world's wealthiest Catholics, the late Princess Grace of Monaco, spent several years trying to persuade the Vatican to annul the marriage of her daughter, Princess Caroline, to Philippe Junot, so that she could regularise her civil wedding to her second husband. The Vatican refused. It could not afford to be seen dissolving a marriage that had taken place in such a glare of publicity.

For ordinary, non-royal Catholics living in Britain, where a civil divorce is relatively easy to obtain, annulment has a purely religious significance. You have to be a devout Catholic (or, like Hans Formella, a professional one) to care about it in the first place. Maeve, in her mid-forties, found the annulment process a relief. 'It hurt to go through it, but at the end, I had come to terms with the breakdown of my marriage. I knew it hadn't been my fault, and that it needn't conflict with my religious beliefs.'

Daniela, however, is critical of the moral basis of the process. 'If I had an annulment, it would effectively declare that my marriage never happened. Although the last few years were awful, I can't dismiss the most important relationship of my life as a non-event. It deserves to be acknowledged. I worked at it hard enough.' Sandra agrees. 'I don't want an annulment. God knows my story. If I ever get married again, it will be in a registry office, and I'll carry on going to communion.'

The fact that an annulment permits them to remarry in a Catholic church is the deciding factor for many people. One couple told us they had waited ten years for their respective annulments to come through. During that time, they had been advised by priests to live together 'as brother and sister', which they found unhelpful and insulting in equal measure. But their mutual longing to bless their relationship in the eyes of God and Holy Mother Church outweighed the indignity of having their sex-lives picked over by clerics.

Many of those present at the ASDC meeting were extremely bitter about the Church which told them marriage was for life, that put them through the suffering of awful relationships, and then ticked them off for getting it wrong. The mere fact of belonging to the ASDC is proof of their religious commitment, but their attitude to the political structure of the Church has become a great deal more sceptical. Their experiences have liberated them and allowed them to make their own decisions through a personal relationship with God, not via a priest. They have, in effect, established their own line to heaven, without going through the Catholic switchboard.

Six:
The
Internal Forum

The difference between what the Church teaches and what certain priests will allow off the record has been one of the recurring themes of this book. Non-Catholics simply see the rules. Catholics know they can shop around for the best deal. This black-market morality is a recognised phenomenon, bearing an official tag, the 'Internal Forum'.

'It's as if you're going about your life and the Church is forever sticking out a leg to trip you up,' says one divorced Catholic, 'and then, when you've fallen on your face, it holds out a helping hand to set you on your feet again.' When you have stumbled over the rule-book, the ministers of the Church show themselves in their best colours, magnanimously kissing it better and assuring you you're all right really. Cynics have pointed out that far from being a sign of undercover liberality, this method is designed to keep erring sheep clinging even more desperately to the hem of the shepherd's cassock.

At the heart of the Catholic faith is the idea of the priest placing himself between the sinner and God. On the assumption that God will shudder at the sight of your filthy sins, the priest gives you a preliminary wipe down in the confessional. As we saw in the opening chapter, Christ's attitude to the woman caught committing adultery shows that any sin is forgivable. In theory, then, confession and the sacrament of penance are very attractive. But, in practice, the Church has institutionalised Christ's generosity and ensured itself power by insisting that in order to be forgiven by God, you must go through a priest.

Protestants, encouraged to have their own private and personal relationship with the Almighty, do not need this com-

155

plicated system of intermediaries. And the dwindling lines out-side confessionals show that many Catholics are coming round to the belief that their sins are between themselves and God, and have nothing to do with the man behind the grille. Only in large city churches, where anonymity is guaranteed, do significant queues form. The traditional notion that you had to be in a state of grace from confession to attend communion has been quietly dropped from modern pulpit oratory. The new generation of post-Vatican II Catholics regard access to the Eucharist as their right, as an expression of their personal bond with God, and not as a boon granted at the behest of a priest.

Old habits die hard, however, and many Catholics still feel that if they fall short of the Church's ideals, they are cut off from communion. An essential element in confession is the promise never to do it again. Where does this leave the gay man living with a partner, the woman on the pill, the couple who have remarried without annulments? Their very lifestyle is caught up in a notion of sin. For such people the Internal Forum, a modified version of confession, is a welcome solution.

Fr Theodore Davey, head of the Department of Pastoral Studies at Heythrop College, London, describes the operation of the Internal Forum in regard to divorced and remarried couples: 'This is simply a technical way of saying that the Church exercises its healing ministry in two ways, either privately or publicly, according to different needs and circumstances. A confessor is consulted privately about a parishioner receiving the sacrament. To help in what is really a question of conscience, some guide-lines have been elaborated in such cases:

1: There is no possibility of reconciliation between the spouses because the marriage has broken down, as demonstrated by the divorce.

2: There is acknowledgement of any responsibility for the failure of the first marriage and repentance.

3: The second marriage has been in existence for some length of time, and there are new responsibilities from this union, such as children who need nurture and security.

4: The partners are doing their best to live in the love of God.

5: Admission to communion should in no way be seen as a questioning of the lifelong commitment which is marriage, and the use of the private or internal forum should be regarded as very exceptional indeed.'[1]

The Church would have you know that it is doing you a huge favour. It is not for one minute advocating any change in the rules. But at least the Internal Forum gives priests the power to help Catholics who feel alienated from the Church because of their lifestyles. Fr Davey is basing his thoughts on Canon 130 of the 1983 Code of Canon Law: 'of itself the power of governance is exercised for the External Forum; sometimes, however, it is exercised for the Internal Forum only, but in such a way that the effects which its exercise is designed to have in the External Forum are not acknowledged in that forum, except in so far as the law prescribes this for determinate cases.'[2] Essentially, this obscure definition is trying to get away from the idea contained in the 1917 Code of Canon Law that the Internal Forum could be equated with conscience, never a popular idea in the Catholic Church.

Individual priests approach this complex legal subject in different ways, as we can see from the debate provoked by Fr Davey's comments. Mgr Patrick Hennessy, the Judicial Vicar for the Leeds diocese, feels that his colleague is being far too lax. 'Recourse to the External Forum must have been attempted first and failed. Otherwise the nature of the Church is seriously damaged.'[3] Fr Davey's remarried couple must have tried for an annulment first and failed for a good reason, before Mgr Hennessy would let them off the hook.

The differences between these two eminent scholars demonstrate the main drawback with the Internal Forum as a tonic for all of Catholicism's ills. It is all things – and nothing – to the men who supposedly operate it, the priests. To illustrate this diversity we talked about the Internal Forum to a random sample of clerics, all of the same vintage (early forties) and all working in busy inner-city parishes.

Fr Peter, in Belfast, was dimly aware of the phrase Internal Forum. He laughed at Fr Davey's idea of running down a checklist when a parishioner in need came for advice and guidance. 'It's all fairly academic for me because I'd never turn anyone away from the sacraments. They don't come through me. They're much bigger than me.'

His compassionate and all-embracing approach was mirrored by Fr Tony, a London priest. He knew a little more of the theological background, but was puzzled by the notion that the Internal Forum was a subject of live debate within church circles. 'It's just jargon for common sense, for pastoral sensitivity,' he said. 'The key to these questions is judgement. What is best for the people involved, what is best for the parish, will scandal be caused?' The notion of scandal is a favourite stumbling block for those who wish to consign the Internal Forum to the ecclesiastical equivalent of Outer Mongolia. They argue that to allow people who have divorced and re-married outside the church to go to communion will scandalise other parishioners. In Fr Tony's experience – and he stressed that the situation may be different in small town parishes – no one takes a great deal of notice. 'When people start talking of others being scandalised, they are usually talking about themselves, but don't want to admit it.'

Against these two liberal and pragmatic voices should be set that of Fr Jack in Brighton who placed his faith in the rigours of canon law. But no code could be complete, he conceded, without its exceptions, and occasionally, rather like the camel squeezing through the eye of the needle, individuals did match the Internal Forum's criteria. 'Once I've exhausted every possible legitimate means of dealing with a situation, but feel that real justice has not been done, then I would look at the option of the Internal Forum.'

Dismissing those clerics who – as he put it – 'wave a magic wand and imagine sin goes away' – he added that he would refer potential cases to fellow priests before coming to a decision. Access to the sacraments then becomes a matter for committees and more than likely leaves candidates bemused and in the cold. Like Mary, a Glaswegian in her forties. Her English Protestant husband became a 'Catholic hater' soon after their wedding, was unfaithful and refused to bring up their five children in the Faith.

158

After fifteen years of unhappiness, she was dumped for another woman. Mary got a divorce but her hopes of a church annulment disappeared when her local priest 'lost' her application. She met another man who loved her, and got on well with the children. He asked her to move in with him. Before agreeing she went to see her priest to ask for dispensation to continue going to the sacraments.

A case for the Internal Forum? Rather more an occasion for a lecture. Mary was told she was living in sin and an adulterer and was banned from the sacrament. 'I remember sitting alone in church every Sunday while my children received communion. I was excluded from one of my daughter's confirmations and felt cut off from my own background and culture. At one point I thought of having a civil wedding and approached the priest again in the hope of a blessing. To do so, he told me, would bring scandal on his parish.'

Life changed dramatically for Mary when Fr Joe arrived as the new parish priest. He told Mary that the length and commitment of her partnership with Ted was greater than that he had seen in many 'legal' marriages. He told her about the Internal Forum and said she could go to communion.

After eight years away from the sacrament, Mary was able to go to the altar rails watched by her whole family. 'I felt like a different person the following week, though deep down I still feel guilty, as if I shouldn't have been there.'

Quite what the Vatican's Rottweiler in charge of orthodoxy, Cardinal Joseph Ratzinger, would think of Fr Joe's decision is, you might imagine, an academic question. Well, beware kind-hearted priests. You can't escape today's version of the Spanish Inquisition.

The Cardinal has recently taken the unusual step for one at the pinnacle of the Church of launching a personal attack on Fr Theodore Davey in the pages of *The Tablet*, a church journal – and a privately owned church journal at that.

Ratzinger quotes from Fr Davey's writings and challenges his view of the Internal Forum in cases like that of Mary and Fr Joe. Take a look at John Paul II's 1981 encyclical *Familiaris Consortio*, says Ratzinger. There the bar on remarried people going to communion was explicitly stated. As well as violating the Church's laws, wrote John Paul on that occasion, any special dispensation for them might lead the faithful 'into error and confusion regarding the Church's teaching about the indissolubility of marriage'.[4]

The Internal Forum therefore, maintains Ratzinger, cannot be used to wipe away a previous marriage. That can only be done by the approved tribunals – there is to be no furtive snipping of Vatican red tape. He refers rather ominously to 'numerous abuses committed under the rubric of the Internal Forum solution'.[5]

So the Internal Forum can hardly be seen as a beacon of hope for those Catholics whose sexual behaviour has put them on the wrong side of the Church's law. As we have seen, this judgement is particularly hard for people who are, in the eyes of society, leading blameless lives. The bureaucracy of the Church means that it is easier to be forgiven for committing a murder than for having a sexual relationship outside marriage.

We do see that, from the Pope's point of view, the Internal Forum presents a problem. It must be vexing to have to push one set of orders at Staff HQ, when your junior officers in the trenches are quietly pushing another. And those Catholics who have taken the trouble to stick to the rules are often annoyed to see someone who has flagrantly disregarded them merrily taking communion with the blessing of the priest.

But they should consider Christ's parable of the labourers in the vineyard (Matt 20), who grumbled at their employer: '"The men who came last have done only one hour, and you have treated them the same as us, though we have done a heavy day's work in all the heat." He answered one of them and said, "My friend, I am not unjust to you. Did we not agree on one denarius? Take your earnings and go. I choose to pay the lastcomer as much as I pay you. Have I no right to do what I like with my own? Why should you be envious because I am generous?"'

The Internal Forum is not a guaranteed solution. The Pope and his law-givers are not keen on it. And it still depends heavily on priest-power. If you are a Catholic who is having sex outside marriage in any form, we certainly advise you to shop around for a sympathetic priest. But even then, be careful. The CND-supporting, ultra-trendy cleric who loves to spout the Church's social teachings may be to the right of St Thomas Aquinas when it comes to sex. And the grizzled old Maynooth tyrant in the biretta may prove unexpectedly broad-minded and kind. You pays your money and you takes your choice, but it is always the priest who has control over your communion with God. Whether his eye is benign or condemnatory, it is still glued to the keyhole of your bedroom door.

Conclusion

The Roman Catholic Church is severely out of step with the sexual customs of our age. No matter how trendily it dresses up its ruling on the subject, the fundamental problem remains – the ancient definition of sex as evil. It is this basic belief that makes emotional and sexual fulfilment an impossible dream for many practising Catholics.

What would happen to the Catholic Church if it declared the sexual act morally neutral? Of course, there would have to be some guidelines for the individual conscience. Sexual activity is wrong when it exploits others – for example, rape and child abuse. It is wrong when it makes another person unhappy, as when a married person has an affair. It is wrong to use sex as an expression of violence or hate. It is wrong to be promiscuous, because – apart from the risk of spreading nasty diseases – you will inflict emotional damage on others.

We cannot see, however, what can possibly be wrong with an exchange of fluids between consenting adults. And, in this overpopulated world, we see absolutely nothing wrong with contraception. If the Vatican decided that there was nothing evil about the act itself, inside or outside marriage, the change would be dramatic. Homosexuals would no longer feel excluded by the Church's condemnation of their sexuality. Children in Church schools would receive realistic and civilised sex education. Married people would be able to enjoy a full, enriching sex-life, without having to worry about conceiving an unwanted child. Those whose marriages had broken could find happiness with someone else, without being destroyed by guilt. Priests would be able to marry, or to live with homosexual partners. God made human love. He programmed most of us with the desire for one special person. Our sexual urges are usually bound up in this desire.

Down the ages, Christianity has made the mistake of separating love from sex. We believe they belong together. And love – all love – comes from God. Love is God, and God is not insulted or degraded by the physical expression of that love. The message of Christ is 'be perfect'. But he knew that nobody can claim to be perfect, and we do not think that by 'perfection' he meant sexual repression.

Once it has jettisoned its sexual strictures, and put sex in its proper context on the league table of other sins, the Catholic Church will be, we believe, revealed in its true glory – as the Church that takes Christ's message to the poor and dispossessed, and blazes out his love to the whole world.

'For it is out of goodness,' says the Congregation of the Doctrine of the Faith, 'in order to indicate the path of life, that God gives human beings his commandments and the grace to observe them: and it is likewise out of goodness – in order to help them persevere along the same path – that God always offers to everyone his forgiveness. Christ has compassion on our weaknesses: he is our Creator and Redeemer. May his spirit open men's hearts to the gift of God's peace and to an understanding of his precepts.'[1]

Notes

Quotations are from authors' interviews, unless stated otherwise.

Biblical quotations taken from the *New Jerusalem Bible* (Darton, Longman & Todd 1985) unless stated otherwise.

Where we have used the term 'Church' we mean the institutional church. Some contemporary ecclesiology will argue that the Church is 'the people of God'.

Preface

1. David Rice *Shattered Vows* (Michael Joseph 1990)
2. Basil Mitchell *The Oxford Illustrated History of Christianity* Ed. John McManners (OUP 1990)
3. Francis Thompson (1859-1907) 'The Hound of Heaven' *Oxford Book of English Mystical Verse* (Clarendon Press 1917)

Chapter One: Catholics and Sex

1. David Lodge *The British Museum is Falling Down* (MacGibbon and Kee 1965)
2. David Rice *Shattered Vows* (Michael Joseph 1990)
3. 'Declaration on Certain Questions Concerning Sexual Ethics' Sacred Congregation for the Doctrine of the Faith 1975 (Catholic Truth Society 1975)
4. David Lodge *How Far Can You Go?* (Secker & Warburg 1980)

5. Michael Hornsby-Smith *Roman Catholic Beliefs in Britain* (CUP 1991)
6. Pope John Paul II 1980 address
7. 'Pastoral Care of Homosexuals' Sacred Congregation for the Doctrine of the Faith 1986 (Catholic Media Office 1986)
8. Tacitus *The Histories* tr. Kenneth Wellesley (Penguin Classics 1964/1984)
9. Mark 12:28–31 (NJB) *see also* Matt 20:34–40
10. St Thomas Aquinas 'On the Perfection of the Spiritual Life'
11. Plato, quoted in *'A History of Western Philosophy'* Bertrand Russell (George Allen & Unwin 1946)
12. Seneca 'Treatise on Marriage'
13. Bertrand Russell *A History of Western Philosophy*
14. Uta Ranke-Heinemann *Eunuchs for Heaven* (Hoffman und Campe Verlag 1988, André Deutsch 1990, tr. John Brownjohn)
15. *The New Jerome Biblical Commentary* ed. Brown, Fitzmyer & Murphy (Geoffrey Chapman 1989)
16. 1 Cor 11, Timothy 2
17. St John Chrysostom 'To the Fallen Monk Theodore' quoted by Marina Warner *Alone of All her Sex* (Weidenfeld & Nicolson 1976)
18. Old Irish Poem, quoted Warner *as above*.
19. Joanne Hayes and John Barret *Joanne Hayes: My Own Story* (Brandon 1985)

Chapter Two: Childhood

1. Alban Butler *Lives of the Saints* 1756–9. Revised edition ed. Thurston and Attwater 1926–38. Concise edition Burns & Oates 1981, ed. Michael Walsh
2. William J. O'Malley 'Teenagers and . . . you know what', *America* 15 April 1989, Vol 160, No. 14
3. Matt 5:8

4. Rupert Brooke 'The Soldier' from *Poems 1914, The Penguin Book of First World War Poetry* ed. Jon Silkin (Penguin 1979)
5. Marina Warner *see* Ch 1 Note 17
6. *see above*, Note 2
7. Gerard S. Sloyan *Catholic Morality Revisited* (Twenty-Third Publications 1990)
8. *Gaudium et Spes, Documents of Vatican II* ed. Austin Flannery (Firepost Books 1975)
9. quoted by Brenda Maddox *The Pope and Contraception* (Chatto & Windus 1991)
10. Thomas Gray 'Ode on a Distant Prospect of Eton College' 1742
11. *Catholic Herald* 27 September 1991
12. *Irish Catholic* 29 August 1991
13. *Irish Catholic* 5 September 1991
14. St Augustine, *City of God* tr. Henry Bettenson (Penguin Classic 1984)
15. Ibid.
16. Ibid.
17. Ibid.
18. *see above* Ch 1 Note 3
19. Bob Geldof *Is That It?* (Sidgwick & Jackson 1986)
20. Philip Larkin 'This be the Verse' / 'High Windows' 1974
21. Daniel Corey 'Family'
22. Ibid.

Chapter Three: Years of Indiscretion

1. *Catholic Herald* 5 April 1991
2. Antonia White *Diaries 1926–57* ed. Susan Chitty (Constable 1991)
3. *Catholic Herald* 5 April 1991
4. Ibid.
5. *see above*, Ch 1 Note 5
6. *The Universe* 18 October 1991

7. *see above*, Note 5
8. G. K. Chesterton *Father Brown*
9. Code of Canon Law 1983
10. *see above*, Ranke-Heinemann Ch 1 Note 14
11. Ibid.
12. *Casti Connubii* 1930
13. The Birth Control Report *The Tablet* 22, 29 April; 6 May 1967
14. Ibid.
15. Ibid.
16. David Rice *see above*, Preface Note 1
17. Ibid.
18. *The Tablet* 4 February 1989
19. Pope John Paul II *Familiaris Consortio* 1981
20. Hornsby-Smith *see above*, Ch 1 Note 5
21. Ibid.
22. Ibid.
23. *Irish Times* 11 March 1991
24. Brenda Maddox *see above*, Ch 2 Note 9
25. Dr Elizabeth Stuart *Roman Catholics and Homosexuality* Channel 4 Television 1990
26. Ibid: the case for the Sin of Sodom being that of inhospitality is convincingly argued here
27. Ibid.
28. *see above*, Ch 1 Note 3
29. Ibid.
30. 'An Introduction to the Pastoral Care of Homosexual Persons' Catholic Social Welfare Commission 1979
31. *see above*, Ch 1 Note 7
32. Ibid.
33. Ibid.
34. Ibid.
35. Ibid.
36. *The Tablet* 23 February 1991
37. *see above*, Note 31
38. Ibid.
39. *see above*, Note 25
40. *Catholic Herald* 6 September 1991

41. Ibid.
42. *The Tablet* 16 February 1991
43. during 1991 trip to US – quoted by Fr Bernard Lynch
44. *see above*, Note 31

Chapter Four: Tending to Perfection

1. St Bernard of Clairvaux quoted by Rice, *see* Preface, Note 1
2. *Vatican Statistical Yearbook for 1989* (published 1991)
3. *Catholic Herald* 19 October 1991
4. Richard Sipe *A Secret World: Sexuality and the Search for Celibacy* (Brunner/Mazed 1990)
5. Fr Richard McKay *Independent on Sunday* 16 August 1991
6. Shalom Ben-Chorin *Mutter Mirjam* (Deutscher Taschenbusch Verlag 1982)
7. Ibid.
8. Baignent, Leigh & Lincoln *The Holy Blood and the Holy Grail* (Jonathan Cape 1982)
9. *see above*, Ch 2 Note 14
10. St Thomas Aquinas *Summa Theologiae: A Concise Translation* ed. Timothy McDermott (Eyre & Spottiswoode 1989)
11. *Catholic Herald* 2 August 1991
12. 1 Cor 7:32
13. *see above*, Preface Note 1
14. Ibid.
15. Ibid.
16. St Teresa of Avila *Life* 1565, tr. J. M. Cohen (Penguin Classics 1957)
17. Shirley du Boulay *Teresa of Avila* (Hodder & Stoughton 1991)
18. *see above*, Note 16
19. *Catholic Herald* 14 September 1990
20. *see* Rice, Preface Note 1
21. Mary Anne Huddleston 'Sex, Sense and the Celibate Priesthood' *America* 1 December 1990, Vol 163, No. 17
22. Ibid.

23. Ibid.
24. Leslie Bennetts 'Unholy Acts' *Vanity Fair* December 1991
25. *The Tablet* 2 February 1991
26. *The Tablet* 2 March 1991
27. Ibid.
28. *see above,* Note 20
29. Ursula Goldmann-Posch *Unheilige Ehen; Gesprache mit Priesterfrauen* 1985
30. Ibid.
31. Ibid.
32. *see above,* Note 20
33. Stuart *see above,* Ch 3 Note 25
34. Marcelle Bernstein
35. Quoted in Rice *see above,* Preface Note 1
36. Ibid.

Chapter Five: Whom God has Joined

1. Piers Paul Read *Quo Vadis* (Claridge Press 1991)
2. Code of Canon Law 1983
3. *Catholic Herald* 27 January 1984
4. *Faber Book of Anecdotes* ed. Clifton Fadiman (Faber & Faber 1985)
5. *see* Christopher Brooke, *The Medieval Idea of Marriage* (OUP 1989)
6. Ibid.
7. *see above,* Ch 4 Note 10
8. *see above,* Ch 2 Note 8
9. Ibid.
10. Mitch Finley 'The Dark Side of Natural Family Planning' *America* 23 February 1991
11. Ibid.
12. Authorised Version of the Bible (HM Printers)
13. *Donum Vitae* Congregation for the Doctrine of the Faith Catholic Truth Society 1987

14. Ibid.
15. William Daniel, S. J. 'Towards a Theology of Procreation; An Examination of the Vatican Instruction *Donum Vitae'* *Pacifica* 3 (1990)
16. *see above,* Note 14
17. Ibid.
18. Office of Population Censuses
19. *Catholic Herald* 20 September 1991
20. 'To Live Without Fear' Canadian Catholic Bishops p 147 13 June 1991
21. Ibid.
22. *Catholic Herald* 21 December 1990
23. *Vatican Statistical Yearbook for 1989*
24. Ibid.

Chapter Six: The Internal Forum

1. *The Universe* 20 October 1991
2. Code of Canon Law 1983
3. *The Universe* 3 November 1991
4. *see* Note 19, Chapter 3
5. Cardinal Joseph Ratzinger, *The Tablet* 26 October 1991

Conclusion

1. *Donum Vitae see above,* Ch 5 Note 15

Index

Main references are in **bold** type

Index